AMERICAN THiNK

STUDENT'S BOOK 4

B2

Herbert Puchta, Jeff Stranks & Peter Lewis-Jones

CAMBRIDGE
UNIVERSITY PRESS

CONTENTS

PRONUNCIATION	THINK	SKILLS		
Diphthongs: alternative spellings	**Train to Think:** Thinking rationally **Self-esteem:** How adventurous are you?	Reading	Article: Sacrifice for survival? Article: The ultimate survivor Photostory: The challenge
		Writing	An email about an experience
		Listening	Radio show: *Desperate Measures*
Phrasal verb stress	**Train to Think:** Distinguishing fact from opinion **Values:** Learning from other cultures	Reading	Article: Refugees bring new life to a village Blog: From Miami to Mexico City Culture: Nomadic People
		Writing	An informal email
		Listening	Radio interview about migration in nature
Adding emphasis with *so, such, do*, or *did*	**Train to Think:** Changing your opinions **Self-esteem:** Developing independence	Reading	Blog: An embarrassing dad Book blurb and reviews: For and Against –Tiger Moms Literature: *About a Boy* by Nick Hornby
		Writing	An essay about bringing up children
		Listening	Radio show about bringing up children in different cultures
Pronouncing words with *gh*	**Train to Think:** Lateral thinking **Values:** Appreciating creative solutions	Reading	Article: Lion lights Web post: A problem on Answers4U Photostory: Writer's block
		Writing	A story ending: *"Thanks, you saved my life!"*
		Listening	Talking heads – being imaginative
The /ə/ sound	**Train to Think:** The PMI strategy **Self-esteem:** Learning from elderly people	Reading	Texts: Smart screens? Article: Great success for teenage teachers: When silver surfers get connected Culture: When pictures learned to walk and talk: The history of film
		Writing	Instructions
		Listening	A conversation about watching too much TV
The /tʃ/ sound: negative auxilliaries + *you*	**Train to Think:** Exaggeration **Values:** Doing good	Reading	Blog: The day people started talking Article: An Ice Cold Summer Literature: *A kind of loving* by Stan Barstow
		Writing	An essay about social media
		Listening	Radio show: *Radio romances*
Intonation: encouraging someone	**Train to Think:** Learning to see things from a different perspective **Self-esteem:** What cheers me up	Reading	Blog: Me, Myself & My Take on the World Web page: QUOTATIONSforWORRIERS Photostory: The contest
		Writing	A short story
		Listening	Radio show: *Silver Linings*
Weak forms with past modals	**Train to Think:** The "goal-setting" checklist **Values:** Lists	Reading	Book review: *The Checklist Manifesto* by Atul Gawande Blog: Andrew's list blog Culture: The New Seven Wonders of the World
		Writing	An essay: A Modern Wonder of the World
		Listening	An interview about why we make lists
The /tən/ word ending	**Train to Think:** Avoiding generalizations **Self-esteem:** Being diplomatic	Reading	Presentation: Life and how to live it Quiz: Are you in control? Literature: *The Remains of the Day* by Kazuo Ishiguro
		Writing	An article for the school magazine
		Listening	A radio show about life choices
Linking: omission of the /h/ sound	**Train to Think:** Identifying the source of a piece of news **Values:** News or not?	Reading	Magazine article: Everybody's Tweeting Article: Bad news Photostory: The news clip
		Writing	A magazine article about an interview with a well-known person
		Listening	An interview with a foreign correspondent
Sentence stress: modals for speculation	**Train to Think:** Spotting flawed arguments **Self-esteem:** Who we are	Reading	Article: They might not come in peace … Blog: My all-time favorite movies about space Culture: Real Humans
		Writing	A report about a problem on a school trip
		Listening	A talk about the Voyager mission
Flapping *t* and *d*	**Train to Think:** Exploring hidden messages **Values:** Human activity and the natural world	Reading	Article: Our undiscovered world Article: Discoverers Literature: *The Lost World* by Arthur Conan Doyle
		Writing	A short biography
		Listening	A talk about discovering new species

WELCOME

A WHAT A STORY!
A lucky pilot

1 🔊 1.02 **Complete the conversation with the verbs in the correct tense. Then listen and check.**

~~crash~~ | hit | find | add | end | pull | keep
take | destroy | scream | manage | dive

MIKE Did you see that story about the plane that
⁰ *crashed* in the Gulf of Mexico?

ANDY No, I didn't. What happened?

MIKE Well, this guy ¹_____ off from Miami in a single-engine plane and headed toward New Orleans.

ANDY Wow. That's a long way.

MIKE Exactly, and it's normally too far for a plane like that, but he had ²_____ extra fuel tanks. After he had begun his journey, however, he realized he didn't have enough fuel to ³_____ on flying, so he radioed New Orleans and told them that he was in trouble and had to land in the ocean.

ANDY In the water?

MIKE Yes, but luckily there was a fishing boat nearby that was able to pick him up. But here's the incredible thing. The plane had a parachute, so the pilot opened it, but this didn't work, and the plane started to ⁴_____ toward the water! Then, almost at the last second, the parachute pulled the plane horizontal, just before it ⁵_____ the water. The impact almost ⁶_____ the plane.

ANDY And the pilot?

MIKE Fortunately, he was OK. He ⁷_____ to get out of the plane and into a life raft from the fishing boat. Then the people on the boat came and ⁸_____ him out of the raft to rescue him. He was fine. I mean, he didn't ⁹_____ up in the hospital or anything. Now experts are trying to ¹⁰_____ out what exactly went wrong.

ANDY Wow – I would have been so scared. I would have ¹¹_____ like crazy!

2 **Read it again. Answer the questions.**

1 Where was the plane flying to and from?
2 Why had the pilot added extra fuel tanks?
3 What did the pilot use to land the plane safely?
4 How was the pilot rescued?

Descriptive verbs

1 **Match the verbs with the definitions.**

☐	1 demolish	a	to hit very hard and break
☐	2 flee	b	to run away quickly
☐	3 grab	c	to destroy completely
☐	4 rage	d	to shout in a high pitch
☐	5 scream	e	to take something quickly
☐	6 smash	f	to hit
☐	7 strike	g	to burn very fiercely

2 **Use the correct form of a verb from Exercise 1 to complete each sentence.**

0 The car went out of control and *struck* a big truck coming in the other direction.

1 By the time the spy was identified, he _____ the country.

2 The house was old and unsafe, so the town _____ it.

3 Come on, we're late! _____ your coat, and let's go!

4 By the time the firefighters got there, the fire _____ for more than 20 minutes.

5 When she reached her car, she saw that someone _____ the windshield with a rock.

6 I _____, but nobody heard me.

Phrasal verbs

1 Complete the sentences about the story. Then read again and check.

1 The pilot _____ from Miami to go to New Orleans.
2 The pilot was OK. He didn't _____ in the hospital.
3 Now they're trying to _____ what went wrong.

2 Choose the correct options.

1 My father *gave up / ended up* smoking five years ago. He feels so much better now!
2 If you're bored, why don't you *put away / clean up* your room?
3 If there's a problem, tell me, and we can *sort it out / blow it out*.
4 Don't stop! We have to *get on / keep on* running to the finish.
5 We're going on vacation next Saturday for the whole month! I'm really *looking forward to / looking into* it.
6 There are good players here, but she's the best. She really *stands out / looks out*.
7 We had to stay home because our car *broke down / blew out*.
8 All the restaurants were full, so we *took up / ended up* buying some food at the supermarket and eating in our hotel room.

Childhood memories

1 SPEAKING Work with a partner. What do you remember about your first trip to a movie theater? (e.g., who you went with, what the movie was, etc.).

2 Read the extract from an autobiography. Which of the things that you remember are mentioned?

3 Read the extract again and answer the questions.

1 What did theaters show at Saturday matinees?
2 Who did the writer go with?
3 Why did they go early?
4 When did the children usually cheer?
5 When did they boo?

Elements of a story

1 Use a word from the list in each space.

plot | set | hero | characters
ending | villain | dialogues

I read a book last week called *Ecuador Escape*. It was a thriller – a kind of detective story. It is ¹_____ in Manta, Ecuador, in the 1800s. The ²_____ of the story is a woman named Vera, who helps many of the other ³_____ escape from a terrible situation – they have been kidnapped by a horrible old man named Campos. He's the ⁴_____ of the story.

Anyway, the book's really good. I thought the overall ⁵_____ was pretty exciting, and it had an unexpected twist at the end. (I won't tell you the ⁶_____, though, in case you want to read the book yourself.) I really liked the ⁷_____, too. The conversations between the different characters sound like real people talking to each other. It's a good read. I'd recommend it.

2 SPEAKING In small groups, discuss an example of each of these from a movie or book.

1 a great hero 3 a great plot
2 a great villain 4 a great ending

Talking about past routines

Think about yourself when you were five years old. What routines did you have? What things did you do? Write five sentences. Then compare with others.

The Saturday matinee

I'm in my 70s now and have loved the movies ever since I was a kid. Back in the 1950s and 60s, movie theaters used to have Saturday matinees. It was wonderful! Every Saturday afternoon, the theater showed movies for kids – only kids. They showed cartoons, Westerns, action movies, and sci-fi features – everything that kids loved back then (and I guess they still do!)

My brother, who was five years older than me, used to take me. We always tried to show up early so we could get seats somewhere in the first few rows. The theater sold candy and popcorn, and we bought as much as we could. We used to sit and watch the movies while stuffing ourselves with food.

We loved the cartoons. Our favorite was always *Tom and Jerry*, and we used to cheer as soon as we heard the theme song start. We also loved action movies. The plots were often terrible, and the acting, too, but we really didn't care. After all, we were kids! We used to boo the villains and cheer the heroes. Some kids used to throw popcorn at the screen when the villain came on – the ushers sometimes tried to stop us, but usually they gave up! The endings were always completely predictable, of course. The heroes always won, and we cheered like crazy when they did!

B AN UNCERTAIN FUTURE
Future plans

1   🔊 1.03   **Read the conversation. Put the phrases (a–f) in the correct places. Then listen and check.**

a   when you graduate
b   get a good degree
c   to start a family
d   and then travel the world
e   then retire
f   before I think about settling down

MOM   So, Greg, have you thought about which colleges you'd like to apply to yet?

GREG   I told you, Mom – I'm not so sure that I want to go to college.

MOM   But if you ¹____, you'll be guaranteed a secure future. You know, in ten years, you could be the manager of a huge company!

GREG   But that's just it, Mom. I don't want to manage a big company, or a small company either. I don't want to spend 40 years doing that, ²____ and wonder where my life went. That's not the future I want.

MOM   So, what are you going to do ³____ then?

GREG   I'm not sure yet. Maybe work, save some money, ⁴____ for a few months, you know, get some life experience.

MOM   Well, that won't do you much good. In this day and age, employers want people with work experience, not travel experience.

GREG   Well, maybe you're right, Mom. But even so, I want some time for myself ⁵____.

MOM   There's nothing wrong with settling down. That's what your father and I did.

GREG   I know, Mom, and that was fine for you and Dad, back in the last century. But the world's different now, and people have such different aims, ideas, everything!

MOM   Yes, I suppose so.

GREG   But don't worry, Mom. I mean, I'd like ⁶____ eventually. So you can look forward to playing with your grandchildren someday – I hope.

MOM   Well, I'm delighted to hear that, Greg!

2   **Mark T (true) or F (false) or DS (doesn't say).**

1   Greg and his mom have talked about college before.
2   Greg's father worked for a big company.
3   Greg definitely wants to travel after he graduates.
4   Greg's mother values work experience.
5   Greg would like to be a father someday.

Life plans

1   **Use the words from the list to complete each sentence.**

graduate | settled | retired | travel | degree
start | career | promoted

1   I intended to _____ the world, but when I got to Brazil, I loved it so much that I stayed.
2   I don't know what to do after I _____ from high school.
3   She got her _____ from Harvard.
4   He worked really hard, and after a few months, he got _____.
5   My grandfather had worked for the same company for 42 years before he _____.
6   A marketing class is a good way to start a _____ in sales.
7   They bought a house and _____ down in the town where they grew up.
8   They feel they don't have enough money yet to _____ a family.

2   **SPEAKING Answer the questions in pairs. Then compare your answers in small groups.**

1   At what age do people usually finish school in your country? Do you think this is the right age? Why or why not?
2   At what age can people retire in your country? Is it the same for men and for women? Do you think this is the right age? Why or why not?
3   Do you need a degree to have a good career? Why or why not?

Past perfect tenses

Complete the sentences with the past perfect or past perfect continuous form of the verb.

1 Greg told his parents that he wants to travel before college.

  A He _____ (think) about it for a long time before he told them.

  B He _____ (plan) to tell them earlier, but he couldn't find a good time.

2 Greg and his mom had different future paths for him.

  A She _____ (dream) that he would become a manager of a huge company.

  B He replied that he _____ (think) about getting some life experience.

Being emphatic: *so* and *such*

1 Complete the sentences from the conversation on page 6.

  1 I'm not _____ sure that I want to go to college.

  2 People have _____ different aims, ideas, everything!

2 Make these statements more emphatic. Use *so* or *such*.

  0 Going to college is a fantastic idea.

    Going to college is such a fantastic idea.

  1 Working in the same job for 40 years sounds terrifying.

    _____

    _____

  2 Traveling is an amazing experience.

    _____

    _____

  3 Deciding to settle down is a huge decision.

    _____

    _____

  4 A boring job must be awful.

    _____

    _____

3 SPEAKING Do you agree or disagree with the statements in Exercise 2? Explain your ideas.

Extreme adjectives

1 Look at the *so/such* statements you wrote in the previous Exercise 2 again. Find words that mean:

  1 really big   _____

  2 really good   _____

  3 really bad   _____

  4 really scary   _____

2 Write the words in the correct places.

hot | delighted | interesting | exciting | huge
terrible | scared | miserable | freezing | awesome
tiny | funny

Gradable adjective	Extreme adjective
1 bad	_____ / awful
2 good	fantastic / wonderful / _____ / amazing
3 _____	fascinating
4 _____	terrified
5 _____	hilarious
6 happy	_____
7 sad	_____
8 _____	thrilling
9 big	_____ / enormous
10 small	_____ / minute
11 cold	_____
12 _____	boiling

3 Complete the mini-dialogues. Use a suitable extreme adjective.

  0 A It's cold in here, isn't it?

    B Yes, it's _____*freezing*_____ !

  1 A Are you happy they're coming?

    B Yes, I'm _____.

  2 A He tells funny jokes, doesn't he?

    B Yes, they're _____.

  3 A This room's small.

    B Small?! It's _____ !

  4 A So, it's good news, right?

    B Yes, it's _____.

  5 A Were you scared?

    B Yes, I was. I was _____ !

  6 A Was the film really that bad?

    B Yes, it was. It was _____.

  7 A Was the roller coaster ride exciting?

    B Yes, it was. It was _____ !

  8 A Be careful. The soup's quite hot.

    B It's more than hot. It's _____.

4 With a partner, write four more mini-dialogues using extreme adjectives from Exercise 2 above that don't appear in Exercise 3.

C HOW PEOPLE BEHAVE
Conversations

1 🔊 1.04 **Listen and match the conversations to the pictures. Write 1–3 in the boxes.**

A

B

C

2 🔊 1.04 **Listen again. Complete the spaces with one word.**

CONVERSATION 1

STEVE What's the matter with you?

MARIA I held the door open for that elderly lady; I let her go through in front of me.

STEVE Yeah. That was thoughtful of you. Very
^a_____.

MARIA But she just walked past me and didn't say thank you. She didn't even look at me! It's so ^b_____, I think.

STEVE Oh, you ^c_____ get so worked up. She was probably just thinking about something else.

CONVERSATION 2

MILLY Hi, Jack. Here are your headphones.

JACK My headphones! So you're the one who took them!

MILLY Yes. Sorry, I should ^a_____ asked you, I know, but …

JACK Well, give them back. You're not ^b_____ to take my things without asking!

MILLY OK. I'm sorry. But you don't have to be so ^c_____ about it.

CONVERSATION 3

JASON I'm really upset. I just heard that Paul, one of my best friends, is going to move to Canada.

SOFIA Oh, that's a shame. But never ^a_____, you have other friends, don't you?

JASON Yes, I know, but I'm going to miss him a lot. He's really fun to ^b_____ out with.

SOFIA Well, you don't ^c_____ to lose touch with him – not these days.

JASON That's right. Maybe my parents will ^d_____ me go and visit him some time.

3 SPEAKING **Work with a partner. What would you have said in these situations if you were:**

● Steve?
● Milly?
● Sofia?

Personality

SPEAKING **Work in pairs. Choose six of the adjectives. For each one, think of something that someone could say or do to show that quality.**

calm | cold | generous | kind | lively
polite | rude | selfish | shy | thoughtful
unfriendly | warm

> *If someone talks to you without smiling or being friendly – well, that's cold.*

Using *should*

SPEAKING **What could you say in the following situations? Use a form of *should* and a personality adjective.**

0 Someone has given you an expensive present.
You shouldn't have spent so much! That was so generous of you.

1 A friend of yours has said something unkind to a mutual friend.

2 Your friend wants to ask someone to dance but is shy.

3 A child doesn't want to let another child play with a toy.

4 Someone is getting angry because another person was rude.

Career paths

1 What jobs do you see in the photos?

2 Read the article quickly and find which of the jobs in Exercise 1 it mentions.

TIPS FOR CHOOSING A CAREER

Choosing a career isn't always easy, but it doesn't have to be the agony that some people make it. Here are our tips to help you make up your mind.

A Don't let other people tell you what to do!
There are always people who want you to become a lawyer, or work in banking, or major in engineering. Listen to them, but remember, it's your life, and it's your decision, so be sure that you're the one who makes that decision!

B Consider what you think you're good at.
It's true that things like salary are important, but don't let financial considerations lead you down the wrong path. Follow your heart and your personality – if you're not very outgoing, don't go for a sales job, even if the pay's good. In the same way, if you don't like work that involves paying lots of attention to detail, think long and hard before you decide to do something like applying to study engineering in college.

C Your first decision isn't forever.
Some lucky people get it right first time – they choose a job, love it, and stick with it. But it isn't always like that. You're allowed to change your mind! On the other hand, it's no good agonizing for years either. Maybe you have three or four possible things you'd like to do. So choose one and try it. If you don't like it, try another one.

D Do something of value.
Some people choose their career simply because they think they'll earn huge amounts of money (although the careers that pay the most also have millions of people who never make it to the top). Generally, however, people get more satisfaction out of their career if they feel they are doing something valuable for others. It doesn't have to be charity work. It could be a job that helps other people, like being a teacher. Just don't forget that job satisfaction isn't only about money.

3 SPEAKING Put the four tips (A–D) in order to show how useful you think each one is. (1 = most useful, 4 = least useful.) Compare your ideas with a partner.

Decisions

1 Complete the questions. The first letter has been given to you.

1 What do you find it difficult to m _ _ _ _ decisions about?

2 When do you think it's wrong to change your m _ _ _ _?

3 Can you remember a time when you couldn't m _ _ _ u _ your mind about something?

4 Who do you talk to before you c _ _ _ _ t _ a decision about something?

5 What kind of things do you think l _ _ _ _ and h _ _ _ _ about before making a decision?

2 SPEAKING Answer the questions in the previous exercise for yourself. Make notes. Then discuss your answers in a group.

Permission

1 Use the correct form of *make / let / be allowed to* to complete the sentences.

1 You should never _____ other people make decisions for you.

2 No one can _____ you do a job that you don't want to do.

3 In more and more jobs now, people _____ work from home if they want to.

4 My mother's boss _____ her work late sometimes.

5 Back when my grandfather worked, he _____ smoke in his office. Can you believe that?

6 This company _____ its employees start work at 8:00, 9:00, or 10:00, whatever works best for them.

2 Write sentences about your perfect job or career. Use *make / let / be allowed to* in some of your sentences.

My ideal company lets all the employees play their own music.

D NEW THINGS
A change of lifestyle?

1 🔊 1.05 **Read and listen to the conversation.**

1 Where are Tom and Isabel?
2 Who doesn't want to be there? Why?

2 🔊 1.05 **Listen again and complete the conversation.**

TOM You said it opened at eight o'clock.

ISABEL And I was wrong! I'm sorry. Don't be so ¹_____ . It'll be open very soon.

TOM I already wish I hadn't come.

ISABEL Oh come on, Tom. We ²_____, didn't we? You said that you were fed up with your ³_____ lifestyle.

TOM True. And then you ⁴_____ me that the best thing to do was exercise.

ISABEL Right. And I ⁵_____ you to come with me to the gym, and you agreed, so here we are.

TOM I always feel ⁶_____ wearing workout clothes. I have skinny legs.

ISABEL Oh, stop complaining, Tom. There's nothing wrong with your legs.

TOM I asked you what I ⁷_____ wear, and you said shorts. But I look terrible!

ISABEL Look, no one cares about what other people look like. They're too busy exercising.

TOM That's completely untrue!

ISABEL Tom, I'm beginning to wish I ⁸_____ invited you. Oh look, it's opening. Let's go in and get started.

3 **Answer the questions.**

1 Why has Tom agreed to exercise?
2 Why is Tom not happy about wearing shorts?
3 Why, according to Isabel, are people not worried about other people's appearance?
4 Why is Isabel starting to regret inviting Tom?

Reporting verbs

1 **Rewrite each sentence. Use the verb in parentheses.**

0 "Please come to my party, Jim." (invite)
She *invited Jim to come to her party.*

1 "You should watch this show." (recommend)
He _____

2 "No, I won't help you, Molly." (refuse)
He _____

3 "I'm late because there weren't any buses." (explain)
She _____

4 "OK, I'll lend you my jacket, Tony." (agree)
He _____

5 "OK, Alice, I'll go to the movies with you." (persuade)
Alice _____

6 "Go on. Ask him, Sue!" (encourage)
I _____

2 **SPEAKING** **Work in pairs. Tell your partner about:**

1 a time someone persuaded you to do something
2 a book or movie that someone recommended to you
3 something you would not encourage another person to do
4 a time when you refused to do something that another person wanted
5 something you once agreed to do and then regretted it

Negative adjectives

1 **Write the negative form of these adjectives.**

1 happy	_____	4 complete	_____
2 patient	_____	5 regular	_____
3 possible	_____	6 legal	_____

2 **Complete the sentences using the negative form of an adjective in the list.**

~~expensive~~ | important | logical
formal | responsible | polite

0 I don't like spending a lot of money. I like to buy *inexpensive* things.

1 It's an _____ party. Wear what you want.

2 The way you dress for school is _____ . It's better to focus on your classes.

3 The way he was explaining the math problem seemed _____ . I didn't understand.

4 My brother never says please or thank you. He's so _____ .

5 You've got an exam tomorrow. It's _____ to stay up so late.

Another country

1 Read the blog. Which of the things in the photographs does Lety not talk about?

Lety's blog – from Bangkok!

Hi everyone,

Well, those of you who read my blog regularly know that I've moved – I'm now living in Bangkok, since my parents got jobs here and they're on two-year contracts, so here we are. We got here about a month ago, and we've found a place to live, so we're starting to settle in.

It's so different from home here. Well, that's unsurprising, of course! For one thing, there's so much traffic all the time, and for a country girl like me, who's used to peace and quiet, it isn't easy to deal with. I guess I'll get used to it, but it might take a while! I just wish someone had told me in advance that it would take me an hour to get from home to school every day – and an hour to get back! But I've made a resolution: I'm going to use my travel time wisely – to learn to knit maybe, but mainly to learn Thai. I think I'm going to struggle because Thai has a different writing system and incredibly difficult pronunciation. But I'm going to put my mind to it, and I hope I can make some progress. (It's a good thing lots of signs are in the Latin alphabet, too; otherwise, I'd be completely lost!) One of my friends told me to try to learn some Thai before coming here – if only I'd listened to him! It'd be a lot easier now I guess.

One of the truly wonderful things here is the food. You may remember that I've already raved about how much I love Thai food. My favorite restaurant at home is Thai, so I'm used to all those spices, and I love them. But here – wow, the flavors are out of this world. Well, that's all for now. I'll write more soon!

2 Read again. What three things does Lety have to get used to?

3 SPEAKING Think of two more possible things that Lety has to get used to. Compare your ideas.

Changes

Use words from the list to complete the sentences.

~~resolution~~ | break | ways | doing well
taking up | struggle | give up | make

0 Lety's made a _resolution_ to use her travel time well.

1 She's thinking of _____ knitting.

2 She thinks she's going to _____ to learn Thai.

3 She's started learning already, but so far she isn't _____ .

4 Moving to another country is a chance to _____ some progress with language skills.

5 I love spicy food, so I could never _____ eating hot peppers.

6 I need to get in shape, so I'll have to change my _____ .

7 I don't think I'm ever going to _____ my bad habits.

Regrets: *I wish … / If only …*

1 Complete the sentences from Lety's blog. Then read again and check.

1 I just wish someone _____ me in advance that it would take me an hour to get from home to school every day.

2 One of my friends told me to try to learn some Thai before coming here – if only _____ to him!

2 Lety wrote some emails to her friends back home. Complete the things she said. Use verbs from the list to help you.

~~say~~ | wear | find | bring | know

0 I didn't see Jack before I left – I wish _I'd said_ goodbye to him.

1 Electronics here are really expensive. If only _____ a little more money!

2 I went to a party last night, and it was really hot. I wish _____ lighter clothes.

3 There are lots of beautiful temples here. If only _____ something about Buddhism before coming here.

4 Our apartment here is really small. I wish my dad _____ a bigger one.

1 SURVIVAL

READING

1   Look at the photos. Can you see *a summit*, *a rope*, *a glacier*, and *a crevasse*?

2   Imagine spending time in an environment like this. What kinds of things could go wrong? What are the dangers? Make a list.

3   ◆)) 1.06   Read and listen to the article to find out what went wrong for two mountain climbers.

4   Read the article again. Seven sentences have been removed
✳ from the article. Choose from the sentences A–H the one that fits each blank (1–7). There is one extra sentence.

   A   Then something dramatic happened.
   B   Simon couldn't talk to him or see him.
   C   Several teams had tried before, but they had all failed.
   D   Both men knew that it would be impossible to survive.
   E   Despite his extreme injuries, he had managed to crawl out of the crevasse.
   F   And they had run out of fuel for their stove.
   G   When he finally arrived at base camp, he was absolutely exhausted.
   H   The weather conditions were awful.

5   SPEAKING   Read what Joe Simpson said in an interview about his relationship with Simon Yates after the event. Then discuss the questions.

In a paradoxical way, in cutting the rope, which nearly killed me – and to his mind, he had killed me – he put me in a position to save my own life, and I owe him the world for getting me into that position … I'd like to say I could have done the same thing. I'm not sure, though. So it was never an issue with Simon and I, and we've been close friends for the last […] 20 years.

1   What do you think of the decision that Simon made?

2   What decision do you think you would have made if you'd been in Simon's position?

3   Joe Simpson is now a motivational speaker whose presentations are very popular. Why do you think this is the case, and would you go to see one of his talks if you had the chance? Give reasons.

Sacrifice for **survival?**

This is the story of two ambitious mountain climbers, Joe Simpson and Simon Yates, whose story was later made into a movie. *Touching the Void.* It started with an outstanding success. Joe and Simon managed to climb the west face of Siula Grande in the Peruvian Andes.

¹____ After reaching the summit, Joe and Simon decided to go back down via the North Ridge, an extremely risky but faster route. Their ascent had already taken much longer than they had intended because of bad weather. ²____ So it wasn't possible for them to melt ice and snow for drinking water anymore. It was getting dark, too, and they knew they needed to descend quickly to the glacier, about 1,000 meters below. ³____ Joe slipped and landed awkwardly, breaking his leg.

Both Simon and Joe were terrified. They were at a height of 6,000 meters. ⁴____ They were freezing. They had no communication with the base camp, and there was no chance of a rescue helicopter or any other form of outside help. The situation was dire, not just for Joe, but for both of them. As an enormous snowstorm was building up around them, Simon tied two ropes together, tied them around Joe, and started lowering his injured friend. Suddenly, the knot got stuck between two rocks, and Joe was left hanging from a cliff, in midair over a huge crevasse.

⁵____ He tried desperately for more than an hour to pull his friend up, but without success. The situation was absolutely hopeless. Simon imagined both himself and his friend dying in the snow and ice. He didn't want to leave his friend alone, but the more he thought about it, the more he began to understand that there was no way he could save both his own life and that of his friend.

For a moment, Simon felt like giving up. But he decided to cut the rope and save his own life. Joe fell away, right down to the bottom of the crevasse. The next day, when Simon continued down the mountain and passed the area where Joe had landed, he saw no signs of life. He assumed Joe was dead.

But he wasn't. Joe had survived the fall. ⁶____ For the next three and a half days, he continued to descend the mountain, crawling and hopping on one leg under extremely difficult conditions. He even managed to cross a glacier with no safety equipment or rope assistance whatsoever.

⁷____ The others were thrilled and amazed to see him, especially because they had been preparing to leave. Joe's incredible determination and the fact that he hadn't given up under the most desperate conditions had helped him to save his own life.

■ TRAIN TO THINK ■

Thinking rationally

Solving a problem requires decision-making. In a difficult situation, it is important not to get distracted by irrelevant ideas so we can concentrate on what is relevant and make the right decision.

1 **Which of these facts were relevant for Simon in making his decision to cut the rope?**

1 Siula Grande is part of the Andes region of Peru. ☐

2 The two climbers had already reached the summit. ☐

3 Joe had a broken leg. ☐

4 There was no way they could get help from anywhere. ☐

5 Their way back down was via the North Ridge. ☐

6 The rope got stuck, and it was impossible to pull Joe out of the crevasse. ☐

2 SPEAKING Work in pairs. Discuss how Simon may have felt when he made his decision.

3 SPEAKING Read the situations. For each one, think about what you might want to do and what you should do. Then compare ideas with a partner.

1 You have an important test tomorrow, and your friend wants you to go to a party tonight.

2 You haven't been feeling well for several days. A tells you to go to a doctor. B tells you to take some medicine. You like B more than A.

3 You borrowed a friend's bike and had a small accident. There's a scratch on the bike that isn't easy to see.

Pronunciation

Diphthongs: alternative spellings
Go to page 120. 🔊

GRAMMAR
Verbs followed by infinitive or gerund

1 **Read the sentences about the article on page 13 and choose the correct words. There are two sentences in which both options are possible. Then complete the rule with *a gerund* and *an infinitive*.**

1 Joe and Simon managed *to climb / climbing* the west face of Siula Grande.

2 Simon tied the rope around Joe and started *to lower / lowering* his injured friend.

3 Simon imagined both himself and his friend *to die / dying* in the snow and ice.

4 For a moment, Simon Yates felt like *to give / giving* up.

5 But then he decided *to cut / cutting* the rope and save his own life.

6 He continued *to descend / descending* the mountain.

> **RULE:**
> We follow the verbs
> - *imagine, feel like, suggest, practice, miss, can't stand, enjoy, detest,* and *don't mind* with [1] _____.
> - *manage, want, decide, refuse, hope, promise, ask, learn, expect, afford, offer,* and *choose* with [2] _____.
> - *begin, start,* and *continue* with [3] _____ or [4] _____ with no difference in meaning.

VOCABULARY
Verbs of movement

1 **Complete the sentences with the correct verbs in the list. Check in the article on page 13.**

crawling | climb | hopping | descend

1 They managed to _____ the west face of Siula Grande.

2 They knew they needed to _____ quickly to the glacier.

3 For the next three and a half days, he continued to descend the mountain, _____ and _____ on one leg.

2 **Match the words with their definitions.**

1 climb	2 hop	3 stagger	4 leap	5 rush
6 crawl	7 wander	8 tiptoe	9 swing	10 descend

a ☐ jump on one foot

b ☐ walk around without any clear purpose or direction

c ☐ move easily and without stopping in the air, backward and forward or from one side to the other

d ☐ walk on your toes, especially in order not to make a noise

e ☐ go or come down

f ☐ go up, or to go toward the top of something

g ☐ (cause to) go or do something very quickly

h ☐ make a large jump from one place to another

i ☐ move slowly on hands and knees

j ☐ walk or move with difficulty as if you are going to fall

2 **Use the verbs in the list to complete the sentences. Use the gerund or infinitive.**

read | help | climb | be | go
walk | get | buy | show

1 The weather was great on Sunday, but I didn't feel like _____ a mountain.

2 I called my friend, and he suggested _____ on a bike ride.

3 Nobody asked us _____ our tickets as we entered the theater.

4 I gave Sarah a copy of Joe Simpson's book *Touching the Void*. She says she's really enjoying _____ it.

5 Can I borrow your umbrella? I can't stand _____ around in the rain.

6 I wanted _____ new skis, but I couldn't afford _____ them.

7 I don't mind _____ my brother with his homework.

8 Can you imagine _____ caught in a snowstorm for hours?

Workbook page 10

3 **Complete the sentences with the correct forms of the verbs from Exercise 2.**

1 They slowly started to _____ into the deep valley.

2 We spent time _____ around the beach looking for shells.

3 I decided to _____ from the rope into the river.

4 The plane _____ to an altitude of 10,000 meters.

5 The baby was sleeping, so they _____ around the house.

6 The boxer managed to _____ to her corner despite being hurt.

7 Some rabbits _____ through the park this morning.

8 When he heard that Jo was back, he _____ over to see her immediately.

9 Our dog _____ through a hole under the fence and ran away.

10 When they saw the rat, they _____ onto the table.

Workbook page 12

LISTENING

1 🔊 1.09 Listen to this radio DJ. What is he giving away? How can a person win?

_____ _____

2 🔊 1.09 Listen again and complete the sentences. Use between one and three words.

1 The callers have 20 _____ to give their answer.
2 The DJ wants the listeners to imagine _____.
3 The caller with the _____ will win.
4 Patty argues that it is always _____ to speak with food in your mouth.
5 Felipe suggests _____ dead when you see a person you want to avoid.
6 Amanda argues that it's your _____ if you get into an awkward situation.
7 She says if you _____ your room, you'll never be in an awkward situation.
8 The DJ thinks Amanda should _____ and get some _____.

GRAMMAR

Different meanings of verb + infinitive and verb + gerund: *remember, try, stop, regret, forget*

1 🔊 1.09 Complete the sentences from the listening with the verb in parentheses. Use the correct form, infinitive or gerund. Listen and check.

1 Remember _____ a snack with you to class. (take)
   I remember _____ to eat a sandwich once in my math class. (try)
2 I regret _____ it because the teacher called my mom! (try)
   I regret _____ that is the craziest idea I've ever heard. (say)
3 If you stop _____ about it, you'll realize it's your own fault. (think)
   Stop _____ ! Go outside and get some fresh air! (talk)

2 Match the sentences and pictures (A–D). Then complete the rule. Write G (gerund) or I (infinitive).

1 She should stop resting, but she just doesn't want to go back to work.
2 She should stop to rest, but she needs to finish her work today.
3 He forgot to meet Sandra.
4 He'll never forget meeting Sandra for the first time.

RULE: *remember, forget, regret*

Remember + ¹_____ means *thinking of a past experience you've had.*

Remember + ²_____ means *don't forget to do something.*

Forget + ³_____ means *to no longer think of something that you did.*

Forget + ⁴_____ means *to not think of doing something you should do.*

Regret + ⁵_____ means *feeling sorry about something you said or did in the past.*

Regret + ⁶_____ means *feeling sorry about something in the future.*

Other verbs

Try + ⁷_____ means *try hard to see if you can do something that is really not easy.*

Try + ⁸_____ means *do it and see what the results are.*

Stop + ⁹_____ means *to not continue doing a certain activity or action.*

Stop + ¹⁰_____ means *pausing one activity in order to do a different activity.*

3 Complete each sentence with the verb in parentheses in the correct form.

1 Before work, Dad stopped _____ some magazines. (buy)
2 I really regret _____ Jim. He's going to tell Martha, I'm sure. (tell)
3 Please remember _____ some paper for the printer. (get)
4 Don't forget _____ the ingredients for the cupcakes, Mom. (buy)
5 Sarah stopped _____ the guitar a few years ago. (play)
6 I just can't solve this puzzle. I've been trying _____ the answer for hours. (find)
7 My ankle hurts. I tried _____ some medicine, but it hasn't helped. (take)

Workbook page 11

VOCABULARY
Adjectives to describe uncomfortable feelings

1 **Read the sentences and ⟨circle⟩ the correct adjectives.**

1 When I'm with Mrs. Meyer, I always feel *awkward / guilty*. It's difficult to find something to talk about with her.

2 Karen ought to be *desperate / ashamed* of herself – talking to her mother like that!

3 Carlos must have done something wrong because he looks so *guilty / puzzled*.

4 After the earthquake, the people on the island were *desperate / awkward* for help.

5 We're a little *stuck / puzzled* as to why we haven't heard from them for weeks.

6 Without your help we'd be *guilty / stuck* and wouldn't know what to do next.

2 **Now write the adjectives from Exercise 1 next to their definitions.**

1 _____ : feeling extremely embarrassed about something you have done

2 _____ : feeling confused because you do not understand something

3 _____ : feeling you are in a difficult situation or unable to change or get away from a situation

4 _____ : feeling embarrassed or uncomfortable

5 _____ : feeling worried or unhappy because you have done something wrong

6 _____ : feeling the need or want for something very much

Workbook page 12

SPEAKING

1 **When you are stuck with a problem, which of these three things apply to you? Add three more of your own.**

☐ I go online and look for some advice.

☐ I stop thinking about it and listen to some music.

☐ I start feeling helpless.

I _____

I _____

I _____

2 **Write down three sentences to describe problems and your emotional reactions to them. Use adjectives from Vocabulary, Exercise 1.**

● *I have a test tomorrow, and I haven't studied enough. I'm really nervous.*

● *It was my best friend's birthday last Monday, and I forgot to give her a present. I'm feeling guilty.*

3 **Work in small groups. Listen to each other's problems and tell each other what to do.**

Stop feeling nervous. Maybe the test won't be very difficult. Just remember to start studying earlier next time.

Try to relax before the test. Listen to some music or go for an early morning walk.

READING

1 **Look at the photos and the headline of the article. Which of these things do you think you could learn from "The Ultimate Survivor"?**

☐ how to build a fire

☐ how to use GPS effectively

☐ how to build a shelter in the wild

☐ how to survive outdoors in bad weather

☐ how to set up your own survival website

☐ how to tie knots

2 **Read the article and check your answers.**

3 **Answer these questions based on your own opinions. Use evidence from the text to support your ideas.**

1 What do you think motivates Bear Grylls?

2 Why are his TV shows so popular?

3 Do you think Bear Grylls is successful? Why?

4 What does Bear Grylls think of the way many young people grow up these days?

The ULTIMATE SURVIVOR

When he was 20, he broke his back in three places in a parachuting accident. He climbed Mount Everest at the age of 23. Shortly afterward he led a trek across the frozen North Atlantic Ocean.

In 2007 he set another world record by flying over Mount Everest in a powered paraglider. This helped to raise one million dollars for the Global Angels Foundation, a charity that supports children in Africa.

His first book, *Facing the Frozen Ocean*, was called an "epic story of hardship, friendship, and faith," by the *Daily Telegraph*. Since then he has authored more than 15 books, including the No. 1 bestseller: *Mud, Sweat, and Tears*.

His name is Bear Grylls, and he was the host of Discovery Channel's famous TV show, *Man vs. Wild*. On the show, he was left stranded in remote locations in order to demonstrate survival techniques. Millions of viewers watched, breathless, as he killed the most venomous snakes and ate them, climbed extremely dangerous cliffs, parachuted from helicopters and balloons, performed amazing ice-climbing stunts, ran through a forest fire, and ate all kinds of insects.

Grylls continues to impress people with his amazing shows and his incredible charity work. He has also set up his own company, Bear Grylls' Survival Academy, where everyone can learn survival skills from him and his team of highly trained experts.

Recently, Grylls founded Young Survivors – training courses for teenagers comprising a combination of survival skills and adventure tasks designed to teach the fundamentals of outdoor survival and self-rescue. Those who complete the course are given a Young Survivors Award. Skills taught include learning priorities of survival, how to build and light a fire, how to navigate in both day and night, building a shelter, extreme weather survival, tracking and hunting, and tying knots. A key focus of the course is getting young people back in touch with nature and away from technology.

In Grylls' own words, "The thing I love about the Young Survivor Course is that it is designed to put young adults in just the sort of challenging, character-building, and practical situations that help define and distinguish people as adults. So often youngsters can feel almost overprotected and are stopped from experiencing some of the best things in life. But the Young Survivor Award will challenge and empower them in an incredibly dynamic and fun environment."

▌THiNK SELF-ESTEEM ▌

How adventurous are you?

1 **SPEAKING** Write a list of some adventurous activities. In pairs, discuss which of the activities from your lists you would like to try (or have tried). Give your reasons.

2 **SPEAKING** Which of the points below are relevant to each of the activities in your list? Discuss.

- [ ] helps you to improve your fitness
- [ ] gets you out of your daily routine
- [ ] teaches you how to assess and deal with risky situations
- [ ] offers opportunities to learn something new
- [ ] offers you a challenge
- [ ] gives you a chance to feel free
- [ ] allows you to have fun with your friends
- [ ] helps you to be more confident
- [ ] teaches you to accept your personal limits

WRITING

An email about an experience

Imagine you are taking a Bear Grylls course. Write an email home to your parents. Tell them:

- about the activities you've been doing.
- how you felt while you were doing them.
- what you've learned from them.
- about the people you've met.
- how you feel about the whole experience so far.

Write 150–200 words.

The challenge

1 **Look at the photos and answer the questions.**

1 What are they all doing in each photo?
2 What do you think "the challenge" is?

2 🔊 1.10 **Now read and listen to the photostory. Check your ideas.**

EMMA What a week this has been!

LIAM I know, right? I have so much to do.

NICOLE Same here. And all of these projects for school. What about you, Justin?

JUSTIN Huh?

EMMA Oh, come on, Justin. You're not listening to us at all.

NICOLE Always on your phone doing something or other.

JUSTIN Sorry. I know it's a bad habit, but whenever someone texts me, I just have to text them back right away.

NICOLE Seems like we're not important to you anymore. You're constantly on your phone.

NICOLE Oh, sorry. Oh, hi, Julia ... Yeah, sure, I'm going ... Yes, we're all going ... No idea, hang on a sec. Let me ask. Guys? When's the Chilly Balloons concert? Is it next week?

JUSTIN On the seventh, nine o'clock.

NICOLE Julia? On the seventh at nine o'clock. ... I'll be home, I guess ... Sure, OK, but not right now ... OK, give me a call over the weekend, and we can talk about it ... OK, bye! ... So, where were we?

JUSTIN Seems like we're not important to you anymore. You're constantly on the phone.

NICOLE Wait a minute – it was Julia, and it was important. She needed help.

EMMA Did you hear that the cheapest tickets to the concert are $60?

LIAM What? That can't be right. Let me check. Here it is – Chilly Balloons, Saturday the seventh, nine o'clock, tickets $35 to $150.

EMMA Oh, that's a relief. Thanks, Liam.

NICOLE You know what? We're yelling at Justin for being on his phone too much, but we're all just as bad.

JUSTIN Ha! True! Hey, I challenge us all not to use our phones for the whole weekend. Not once. I bet you can't do it.

NICOLE Ridiculous. Of course we can. Why wouldn't we be able to?

EMMA Three days without a phone? No problem.

JUSTIN So prove it. Let's make a bet: Anyone who uses their phone has to treat the others to coffee or whatever they want at the café. OK?

EMMA OK. I'm in.

JUSTIN No phones, right up to Monday morning, starting now. Deal?

ALL Deal!

DEVELOPING SPEAKING

3 Work in pairs. Discuss what happens next in the story. Write down your ideas.

We think that two of them succeed and two of them don't.

4 ◼ EP1 Watch to find out how the story continues.

5 Answer the questions.

1 Why does Nicole's dad think she doesn't answer her phone?

2 What did Emma do that means she lost the challenge?

3 What did Liam do or not do about the challenge?

4 How long did Justin manage to not use his phone for?

5 What did Nicole do which means she didn't win the challenge?

PHRASES FOR FLUENCY

1 Find these expressions in the story. Who says them? How do you say them in your language?

1 Same here.   _____

2 something or other _____

3 give me a call   _____

4 Where (were we)?   _____

5 You know what?   _____

6 (It's a) deal!   _____

2 Use the expressions in Exercise 1 to complete the dialogues.

1 A I was really busy over the weekend. No time to relax! I always had _____ to do.

  B _____ ! I didn't stop for a moment.

2 A Listen, if you find the math homework difficult, _____ and I can help you. Then maybe you can help me with English later.

  B _____ ! Thanks a lot, Georgia.

3 A This exercise is exhausting.

  B You're right. _____ ? We should have a break.

4 A So I told him that I thought …

  B Sorry, let me answer this phone call. … Sorry. OK, _____ ?

WordWise
right

1 Look at these sentences from the photostory and video. Complete them with phrases from the list.

… right? | right away | I know, right?
right up to | All right! | Yeah, right.

1 I just have to text them back _____ .

2 A What a week this has been!

  B _____ I have so much to do.

3 No phones, _____ Monday morning. Deal?

4 You know my friends Emma, Justin, and Liam, _____

5 _____ We have a winner!

6 _____ You just loved spending all weekend working on your project.

2 Complete the sentences with a phrase using *right*.

1 You're the new girl at school, _____

2 The party was great. I stayed _____ the end.

3 There's a problem at home. I need to leave _____ .

4 _____ I want you all to listen!

5 A That movie was terrible.

  B _____ I hated it, too.

6 A I can help you with your math homework.

  B _____ You're worse at math than I am!

> Workbook page 12

FUNCTIONS
Making and accepting a challenge

1 Read the phrases. Which ones are used to challenge people? Which ones are used to accept or turn down a challenge?

1 I bet you can't …

2 I think you're right.

3 I bet (you) I can …

4 That's impossible!

5 I challenge you to …

6 No way!

7 You'll never manage to …

8 Of course I can.

2 Work in pairs. Write short dialogues between two people where one challenges the other. Use these ideas and one of your own.

- eat a donut without licking your lips
- stay awake for 24 hours
- walk 20 kilometers in four hours
- finish this exercise before me
- speak only in English during breaks and lunchtime for a whole week

2 GOING PLACES

OBJECTIVES

FUNCTIONS: expressing surprise
GRAMMAR: relative clauses (review);
which to refer to a whole clause;
omitting relative pronouns;
reduced relative clauses
VOCABULARY: groups of people;
phrasal verbs (1)

READING

1 Imagine you are going to live in another country. What things do you have to get used to? Add two more things to this list. Then put the six things in order of difficulty for you (1= most difficult).

the climate	☐	the language	☐
the food	☐	_____	☐
local customs	☐	_____	☐

2 SPEAKING Compare your ideas with other students.

3 SPEAKING Work in pairs or small groups. Look at the photos and these phrases from the article. Discuss what you think the article is about.

- a shortage of jobs
- the creation of workshops
- welcoming of refugees
- the renovation of houses

4 🔊 1.11 Read and listen to the article and check your ideas.

5 All of these statements are incorrect. Read the article again and find the lines that show they are incorrect. Then correct the sentences.

1 Many people in the 1990s left Riace because they didn't like it anymore.
2 The refugees didn't have to do anything to get food and accommodation.
3 The refugees already spoke Italian.
4 New houses were built for the refugees.
5 About a hundred immigrants live in Riace now.
6 More local people are leaving Riace.
7 Many politicians have criticized Lucano's ideas.
8 Lucano won the 2010 "World Mayor" award.

6 SPEAKING Work with a partner and discuss the questions.

1 What two questions would you like to ask
   a a resident born in Riace?
   b an immigrant living and working in Riace?
2 Do you think things will continue to go well in Riace in the future? Why?

Refugees bring new life to a village

Riace is a small village in Calabria, which is a very pretty region of Italy but also a very poor one. Riace once had a population of 3,000, but in the 1990s a shortage of jobs meant that many of the residents, especially young people, left the village to find work in other places. The only school closed. There were no restaurants and very few stores. Many houses were empty. Riace was becoming a ghost town. But these days it's a different story because of one man whose dreams have turned Riace into a village with a future.

One day in 1998, Domenico Lucano, a teacher from Riace, was driving near the sea when he saw a large group of people on the beach. They were refugees who had arrived by boat to escape problems in their countries. Lucano had an idea of how to help these people and how they, in turn, might possibly help him save his village. He decided to welcome them into the village and to give them food and accommodation in return for work. The refugees also had to learn Italian.

It was the beginning of a plan. Lucano created an organization called *Città Futura*, or "City of the Future." The idea was simple: Riace desperately needed more residents, and there were plenty of people in the world looking for a home. The village began to welcome refugees from Somalia, Afghanistan, Iraq, Lebanon, and other places. Lucano used buildings that had been empty for years to house the new arrivals, and he created workshops for them to work in.

Riace is now home to between two and three hundred immigrants, who live happily alongside the locals. Most of the women make handicrafts to sell in local shops, while the men renovate empty houses to rent to tourists. But it is not only the refugees who have gained from Lucano's plans: *Città Futura* also has 13 local employees, which makes it the biggest employer in the village. Because of the arrival of more children, the school is open again, too. Lucano, who became the mayor of Riace in 2004, has managed to create jobs and to stop the villagers from moving away, while at the same time helping some of the poorest and most desperate people in the world.

Many politicians have visited Riace hoping that they can use Lucano's ideas in their own towns and cities. The German film director Wim Wenders also went there and was inspired to make a short documentary about the village called *Il Volo* (*The Flight*). Lucano himself came in third in the 2010 World Mayor contest and was praised for his courage and compassion.

■TRAIN TO THiNK■

Distinguishing fact from opinion

People often have disagreements because they confuse opinions with facts. A fact is something true for which there is usually proof. An opinion is a thought or belief and may not be true. When you want to know if what someone is saying is really true, it's important to ask the right questions to help you separate opinions from facts.

1 **Read the two statements (A). What is the purpose of the question (B) that follows each of them?**

1 **A** *Teenagers never want to travel anywhere with their parents.*

B Does that mean that there has never been a young person who liked traveling with their parents?

2 **A** *I'm convinced listening to music keeps you healthy.*

B What evidence is there that supports that?

2 **Here are things people said to Domenico Lucano when he was about to start his project. Work in pairs and find good questions that he could ask to separate opinions from facts.**

1 All the young people are moving away. Our town has no future.

2 I'm sure these refugees are troublemakers.

3 Don't invite these people to our village. They're poor and will only create problems.

4 It's a bad idea to put people from different countries together. They'll start fighting.

5 These people can't survive in our village. There's just no work for them.

GRAMMAR
Relative clauses (review)

1 **Read the sentences from the article about Riace. Look at the underlined parts. Then complete the rule by writing A, B, C, or D.**

A Riace is in Calabria, <u>which is a very pretty region of Italy</u>.

B Lucano used buildings <u>that had been empty for years</u> to house the new arrivals.

C They were refugees <u>who had arrived by boat</u>.

D Lucano, <u>who became mayor of Riace in 2004</u>, has managed to create jobs.

> **RULE:** We use a defining relative clause to identify an object (*which / that*), a person (*who / that*), a place (*where*), or a possession (*whose*). Without this information, it's hard to know who or what we're talking about. (e.g., [1]_____ and [2]_____)
>
> We use a non-defining relative clause to add extra information. We don't need this information to understand the sentence. We put commas around it. (e.g., [3]_____ and [4]_____)

2 **SPEAKING** **Complete each sentence with *who*, *which*, or *that*. Are they defining or non-defining relative clauses? Then decide if you agree with each statement or not, and discuss with a partner.**

1 I don't understand people _____ decide to live in another country.

2 Sometimes people don't like the new people _____ come to their town.

3 I'd like to live in a country _____ has a different culture from mine.

4 Sometimes it's just a person's appearance _____ makes us like them or not.

3 **Join the sentences to make one sentence by including a non-defining relative clause. Put commas in the correct places.**

0 The people were tired. They had come a long way.

The people, who had come a long way, were tired.

1 The locals gave them food. They were kind.

2 Rome is an exciting place. It is my favorite city.

3 I've been reading a book by Carlos Fuentes. Fuentes is one of my favorite writers.

4 My neighbor Ruben has been living here for ten years. Ruben is from Guatemala.

which to refer to a whole clause

4 **Read the two sentences from the article. What does *which* refer to in each sentence?**

1 Riace is a small village in Calabria, **which** is a very pretty region of Italy.

2 *Città Futura* has 13 local employees, **which** makes it the biggest employer in the village.

5 **Underline** what *this* refers to in each of the second sentences below. Rewrite the sentences as one sentence.

0 A lot of <u>tourists visit</u>. This is good for the town.

A lot of tourists visit, which is good for the town.

1 Some people go and live in another country. This is not always easy.

2 You have to learn new customs. This can be challenging.

3 Some people are nervous about strangers. This makes life difficult for new arrivals.

4 Sometimes there are differences in culture. This often results in misunderstandings.

Workbook page 18

VOCABULARY
Groups of people

Complete each sentence with a word from the list.

~~the audience~~ | pedestrians | residents
the crew | employees | employers
immigrants | politicians | refugees
drivers | the staff | inhabitants

0 People who watch a play / movie / concert are *the audience* .

1 People who walk on a street are called _____ .

2 A group of people who work on a plane or ship are _____ .

3 _____ are people that have a home in a specific place.

4 People who are paid to work for other people are called _____ .

5 People who work in politics are called _____ .

6 _____ are people who leave their own country because it's too difficult or dangerous to live there.

7 _____ pay others to work for them.

8 _____ are people who come to a different country to live there permanently.

9 A group of people who work for an organization are _____ .

10 People who operate cars or trucks are called _____ .

11 People who live in a particular place are the _____ .

Workbook page 20

LISTENING
Migration in nature

wildebeest **A**

Arctic terns **B**

gray whales **C**

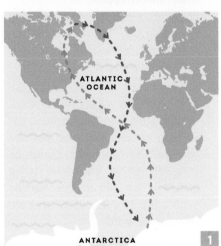

1

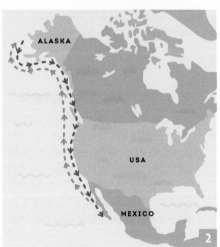

2

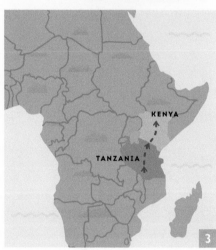

3

1 `SPEAKING` Look at the photos and the maps. Which animals in the photographs make which journeys in the maps? Discuss your ideas.

2 `1.12` Listen to a radio interview. Check your ideas. Write 1, 2, and 3 in the boxes.

3 `1.12` What do these numbers refer to? Listen again and check.

1 18,000	3 2,000	5 70,000
2 more than a million	4 250,000	6 2,000,000

4 `1.12` Correct these sentences. Listen again to check.

1 Gray whales swim to Alaska to have their babies there.
2 Gray whales can be found near Alaska in the winter.
3 The Mara River is at the beginning of the wildebeest's journey.
4 The Mara River is full of whales.
5 Arctic terns do their journey only once in their lifetime.
6 People know how the terns always arrive at the same place.

5 `SPEAKING` Work in small groups. Answer these questions.

1 Which of the animal facts you heard do you think is the most interesting?
2 Do you know about any other animals or birds who undertake amazing journeys?

FUNCTIONS
Expressing surprise

1 `1.12` Listen again to the radio interview. What phrases are used to express surprise? Can you think of any other phrases?

1 _____ (distance)!
2 _____ Unbelievable.
3 It's _____, isn't it?
4 _____ astounding.
5 That's _____

2 Work in AB pairs. A thinks of something surprising. (You can invent something if you want!) A gives the information to B. B uses one of the expressions in Exercise 1 to reply and asks a follow-up question. Then A and B change roles.

Becca's Blog: From Miami to Mexico City

Five not-so-good things about living abroad

Regular readers of my blog already know that I'm a student living and studying in Mexico for a year. Overall it's turning out to be a great experience. But today I've decided to share some of the challenges that living abroad can bring about. Here we go.

 ## A It's no vacation

You know those Hollywood movies where the foreigner is living a nice, easy, comfortable life in another country? Well, forget it. You have to do all kinds of things like open a bank account, find somewhere to live, pay bills, and so on. These things aren't easy, and they take time.

 ## B Language problems

Before I came, I thought my Spanish was pretty good. But speaking it here isn't like speaking it in school. People talk to me like they talk to each other – fast! There's new vocabulary that you have to pick up. The first time I went to a hairdresser, I didn't know what to say! Speaking Spanish all day wears me out. Often, at night, I'll watch anything on TV in English! Anything!

 ## C You might not like it

It's possible that after all the excitement of moving to another country, you become one of those foreigners who is unhappy abroad. I ran into some people who couldn't wait to leave Mexico after just a few weeks. Well, there's no country in the world that suits everybody, right? It's always a risk.

 ## D Homesickness

After a few weeks you'll start to miss all kinds of things (and people) from back home – that special food, that TV show, the friends you used to hang out with. Well, it's a phase you have to go through. If you're really homesick, go home. Otherwise, keep going; the homesickness won't last forever.

 ## E Not everyone is happy that you're there

Most people are kind to me. But there are exceptions. Sometimes I go somewhere, and someone says something like, "Oh, no, not another American!" It's not nice to hear, but you have to put up with it.

Still, overall, I'm very happy to be here, and I have no regrets at all about coming. Sure, there are problems, but you can run into problems wherever you are. The experience gained by living abroad is invaluable. Living abroad is fun and a huge learning opportunity, too. It's made me more aware of the world.

READING

1 **Look at the photo and the title of the blog, and make notes on the following.**

   1 Where do you think the woman is?
   2 Where do you think she's from?
   3 What is this blog entry about?

2 **Read the blog and check your ideas.**

3 **Read the blog again and answer the questions.**

   1 What is Becca doing in Mexico?
   2 Why does she say that it's "no vacation"?
   3 Why is she sometimes tired at the end of the day?
   4 How were some other foreigners different from her?
   5 How does she suggest dealing with homesickness?
   6 How does she deal with comments about her that she doesn't like?

VOCABULARY
Phrasal verbs (1)

1 **Complete these sentences about the blog. Use the correct form of the phrasal verbs from the list. Then go back to the blog to check your answers.**

put up with | bring about | run into | turn out
hang out with | pick up | go through | wear (me) out

   1 You have to _____ a lot of new vocabulary.
   2 Being homesick is a phase that you have to _____ .
   3 It's not nice to hear negative comments, but you have to _____ them.
   4 Sometimes you miss the friends you used to _____ .
   5 Speaking another language all day _____ .
   6 Living abroad is _____ to be a great experience for me.
   7 I _____ some people who wanted to leave Mexico.
   8 Living abroad can _____ some challenges and difficulties.

> **Pronunciation**
> Phrasal verb stress
> Go to page 120. 🔊

2 **Write the correct phrasal verb next to its definition.**

0	make (someone) very tired	*wear out*
1	meet by chance	_____
2	learn (informally)	_____
3	tolerate	_____
4	experience (a difficult situation)	_____
5	have a particular result	_____
6	spend time with	_____
7	make happen	_____

3 **Answer the questions.**

1 Where do you like to hang out? And who with?
2 What wears you out?
3 Have you ever run into a teacher outside school?
4 Can you think of any habits someone you know has that you have to put up with?
5 What difficulties do people go through when they graduate from high school and start college?
6 Do you think it's possible to pick up new words by listening to songs in English?

> Workbook page 20 ▶

GRAMMAR
Omitting relative pronouns

1 **Read the two sentences from the blog. Where can you put a relative pronoun in each sentence? Are these pronouns the subject or the object of the relative clause? Complete the rule with the words *subject* and *object*.**

1 It's a phase you have to go through.
2 You start to miss … the friends you used to hang out with.

> **RULE:** When the relative pronouns *that / which / who* are the [1]_____ of a defining relative clause, they can be omitted. When they are the [2]_____ of the defining relative clause, they can't be omitted.

2 **Read these sentences. Put a check (✓) if you can omit the pronoun in *italics* or an X (✗) if you can't omit it.**

1 I ran into some people *who* couldn't wait to leave. ☐
2 I've decided to share some of the challenges *that* living abroad can bring about. ☐
3 You become one of those foreigners *who* is unhappy abroad. ☐
4 There's new vocabulary *that* you have to pick up. ☐
5 There's no country in the world *that* suits everybody. ☐

Reduced relative clauses

3 **Read these sentences. Where could you put the words *that is* and *who is*? Then check the correct box in the rule.**

1 I'm a student living and studying in Mexico.
2 The experience gained by living abroad is invaluable.

> **RULE:** When relative clauses begin with a relative pronoun + the auxiliary verb *be*, we can omit:
> A ☐ only the relative pronoun
> B ☐ the relative pronoun + the verb *be*

4 **Cross out the words / phrases in *italics* than can be left out.**

Baseball players [1]*who* come from other countries to play in the U.S. often have problems. Some of the players [2]*who are* playing in the U.S. can sometimes feel homesick. And then there are things like food – people [3]*who were* brought up on spicy food or exotic fruit don't always like typical American food. But the biggest problems [4]*that* they face seem to be the weather and the language. The countries [5]*that* they come from might have warm weather all year, which most of the U.S. doesn't. It isn't always easy for players [6]*who* come from Brazil or Mexico, for example, to adapt to the snow and cold [7]*that* they experience in the U.S. And not all the foreign players learn English very well – the ones [8]*who* do, tend to find it easier to adapt.

> Workbook page 19 ▶

▮ THiNK VALUES ▮

Learning from other cultures

1 **Imagine you live in another country. Put the things in Becca's blog (A, B, C, D, E) in order (1 = the most difficult, 5 = the least difficult).**

1 ☐   2 ☐   3 ☐   4 ☐   5 ☐

2 **Choose the options that are true for you in these statements. Make notes about your reasons.**

1 *I'd like / I wouldn't like* to visit other countries.
2 *I'd like / I wouldn't like* to live in another country.
3 *I'm interested / I'm not interested* in other cultures.
4 Knowing about other cultures *helps / doesn't help* me understand my own culture.
5 *I think / I don't think* studying abroad really helps you understand a language.

3 **SPEAKING** **Compare your ideas with the class. How similar or different are you?**

Culture

1   Look at the photos. What do they all have in common?

2   🔊 1.15 Read and listen to the article and check your answers.

Nomadic People

Most of us are used to living in the same place – every day, all year round, we go "home." But for some people around the world, home is a place that moves. Here are three groups of people who have a nomadic way of life.

A The Tuareg

In the central part of northern Africa, which is mostly desert, you can find the Tuareg people, who call themselves *Imohag*, meaning "free people." Most of the Tuareg people are found in Mali, Niger, and Algeria, although some can also be found in Libya and Burkina Faso. Being nomadic people, however, they regularly cross national borders.

They have their own language (Tuareg), which is spoken by around 1.2 million people, but many Tuareg people also speak Arabic and/or French. The Tuareg people are mostly Muslim, although some traditional beliefs remain from before the arrival of Islam.

In the past, the Tuareg moved around the desert areas with their cattle, mainly between places where water could be found. Due to the formation of new countries and stricter borders, severe droughts, and urbanization, nomadic life became more difficult in the 20th century. This led many Tuareg people to settle in towns and cities.

Sometimes the Tuareg are called "the blue people of the Sahara" because of the blue turbans that the men wear, which often gives their skin a blue color.

B The Shahsavan

This tribe lives in an area of northwest Iran and eastern Azerbaijan. There are approximately 100,000 people in it. In the spring the Shahsavan move from their winter home in Azerbaijan to their camps near Mount Sabalan, about 200 kilometers south, for the summer. Their journey usually takes three or four weeks. Each day they travel from midnight to noon, after which the heat prevents travel. Traditionally, the women and children traveled on camels, and the men rode horses or walked, but increasingly the Shahsavan are using trucks and tractors.

When they reach their destination, everyone (including children) is involved in setting up the main camp, consisting of various types of tents. They stay there until September, when the return journey begins.

Many of the Shahsavan believe that their way of life is dying out, that their grandchildren will not do the annual migration anymore.

C Aborigines

The Aboriginal people of Australia have been living there for 40,000 years, since long before Europeans arrived. But they are not one single group – for example, there are more than 200 different languages spoken by the Aborigines.

The Aborigines are hunters and gatherers, almost always on the move. Principally it is the women who gather food and care for the children, while the men are the hunters. They have very few possessions, and the ones they have are mostly light, since they need to keep moving in search of food and to maintain a balanced diet (they eat seeds, fruit, and vegetables as well as small animals, snakes, and insects).

Occasionally, however, groups or families of Aborigines decide to settle in a place and form villages.

3 According to the article, which group (A, B, and/or C):

1 only travels twice a year? _____
2 doesn't own many things? _____
3 speaks more than one language? _____
4 sometimes creates villages? _____
5 moves from one country to another? _____
6 has seen their lifestyle change? _____

4 VOCABULARY Match the highlighted words in the article to the definitions.

1 places where one country ends and another begins _____
2 on a journey or trip, the place you want to get to _____
3 all the things that you eat _____
4 times when there is little or no rain _____
5 mainly _____
6 things that people have and keep _____
7 happening once every year _____
8 stay, continue _____

SPEAKING

Work with a partner. Discuss the following questions.

1 Do you know of any other groups of people who are nomadic? What do you know about their culture?
2 What might be the advantages and disadvantages of a nomadic lifestyle?
3 The article says that many of the Shahsavan believe that their grandchildren won't live in the same way. Why do you think that might be?

Hi James,

How are you doing? Hope you're OK!

Well, here I am at last – living in northern Canada with the nomadic Inuit people. You know that I've been wanting to do this for years, and my dream has finally come true. I'm so excited to be here.

I got here ten days ago and met a family who said I could go along with them to hunt. I've already done some amazing things – sleeping in an igloo, for example, and watching the Inuit people go hunting for fish and for small animals.

The most difficult thing to deal with, of course, is the cold. There's also the fact that you have to keep moving every few days to find food. The way they hunt is interesting. The Inuit make a hole in the ice and hope that a seal will appear so that they can catch it. I went hunting with my host dad a couple of days ago – he showed me how to make a hole and then we stood for six hours in the freezing cold, waiting for a seal to appear. It never came. I got so fed up. But then I thought, hey, the Inuit people do this every day, sometimes waiting for ten hours. And sometimes they catch a seal, and sometimes they don't. What's my problem? What amazes me most about them is their patience, and my own is getting lots better!

Well, I'll write and tell you more about how I'm doing when I can. Hope you're well!

All the best,

Karen

WRITING
An informal email

1 **Read Karen's email and answer the questions.**

1 How long has she been with the Inuit people?
2 When did she try to catch a seal?
3 What does she say is most impressive about the Inuit?

2 Underline the informal words or phrases in the email that mean:

1 a great deal
2 I have finally arrived
3 agreed that I could accompany them
4 I am extremely happy
5 my experiences here
6 one or two days ago

3 Imagine you are spending two weeks living with one of the nomadic tribes mentioned in the article.

- Choose which of the three groups you are living with.
- Decide what things in general have been good / not so good about your experiences so far.
- Decide on one specific thing about their life that has really impressed you.

4 You're going to write an email to an English-speaking friend.

- Make sure to start and end your email appropriately.
- Talk generally about your experiences first. Then move on to more specific details.
- Write 150–200 words.
- Check your writing to make sure that your language is informal.

READING AND USE OF ENGLISH
Part 4: Key word transformations

Workbook page 17 ➔

1   For questions 1–6 complete the second sentence so that it has a similar meaning to the first sentence, using the word given. Do not change the word given. You must use between two and five words, including the word given. Here is an example (0).

0   I think taking the 8 p.m. train is the best idea.
   PREFER
   I'd _prefer to take_ the 8 p.m. train.

1   I've been studying all day, and I'm really tired.
   OUT
   Studying all day has really _____ .

2   I wish I hadn't gone to bed so late.
   REGRET
   I _____ to bed so late.

3   I got really annoyed by Paul and Dave laughing all the time.
   WHICH
   Paul and Dave kept laughing, _____ me.

4   I don't know how you tolerate him.
   PUT
   I don't know how you _____ him.

5   Oh no! I didn't mail her birthday card on the way home.
   FORGOT
   I _____ her birthday card on the way home.

6   Getting up early in the morning is the worst thing.
   STAND
   I _____ up early in the morning.

WRITING
Part 2: An article

Workbook page 25 ➔

2   You have seen this announcement in an international magazine.

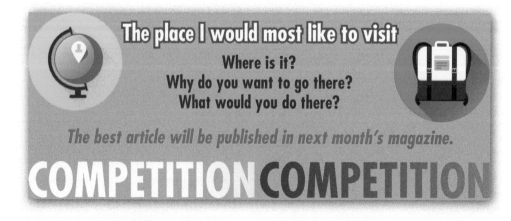

The place I would most like to visit
Where is it?
Why do you want to go there?
What would you do there?

The best article will be published in next month's magazine.

COMPETITION COMPETITION

Write your article in 140–190 words.

VOCABULARY

1 Complete the sentences with the words in the list. There are four extra words.

refugees | turned out | wandering | puzzled | stuck | residents | guilty
employees | rushing | go through | immigrants | ran into | worn out | crawl

1 Sally was _____ slowly around the store looking for a present for her mom's birthday.

2 I hadn't seen Marie for ages, but yesterday I _____ her at the movie theater.

3 I saw a documentary about _____ fleeing across borders to escape the war.

4 I'm so happy that I passed my driving test. It was awful, and I wouldn't want to _____ that again!

5 You haven't done anything wrong. You don't have to feel _____ about anything, OK?

6 Mr. Sawyer runs a small business. He has four _____ who work for him.

7 They are all local _____. Most of them live on the streets near us.

8 My little sister can't walk yet, but she can _____ really fast!

9 I was _____ by my friend's reaction. I couldn't understand why she laughed.

10 The beginning of the show was very sad, but it all _____ well in the end. **/10**

GRAMMAR

2 Complete the sentences. Use the verbs in the list, either with *to* + infinitive or with a gerund (*-ing* form). Use two of the verbs twice.

do | go | live | fall

1 Yesterday my friends decided _____ to the beach to play volleyball.

2 My brother says he remembers _____ out of bed when he was two years old.

3 Jack always forgets _____ his homework and then gets in trouble.

4 I want _____ in a little apartment in Paris one day.

5 I don't mind _____ the dishes at home.

6 I hate being in an empty house. I can't imagine _____ alone.

3 Find and correct the mistake in each sentence.

1 I really like that guy which plays Sam on TV.

2 My brother Julian that lives in New York is coming to visit.

3 It isn't a movie makes everyone laugh.

4 The man what plays the drums in the band is over there.

5 He broke my phone, what means he has to buy me a new one.

6 She's the runner won the gold medal.

/12

FUNCTIONAL LANGUAGE

4 Choose the correct options.

1 A Next week Rebecca's going to run a 15-kilometer race. That's *quite a / really* distance.

   B Yes, it is. And she only started running a month ago, too. That's *amazing / awful*.

2 A I heard that you got 95 percent. That's *OK / unbelievable*. Well done!

   B Thanks. I could hardly believe it. And my parents thought it was *incredible / quite*. **/8**

3 A *I'm betting / bet* you can't say "Good morning" in five different languages.

   B Well, you're right – I *can / can't*.

4 A You *can / will* never manage to stay off the Internet for two days.

   B Mm, I think you're right, but I *challenge / can challenge* you to stop using email for a week!

MY SCORE **/30**

22 – 30
10 – 21
0 – 9

3 THE NEXT GENERATION

OBJECTIVES

FUNCTIONS: emphasizing
GRAMMAR: quantifiers; *so* and *such* (review); *do* and *did* for emphasis
VOCABULARY: costumes and uniforms; bringing up children

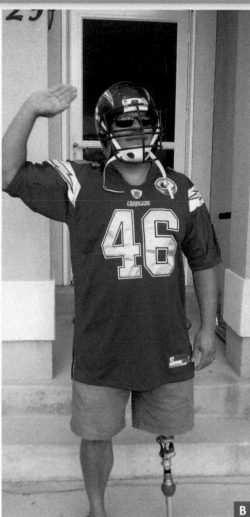

READING

1 **Look at the photos and match them with the captions.**

- [ ] King for a day
- [ ] Go Chargers!
- [ ] Kiss the chef
- [ ] Batman and Boy Wonder

2 **SPEAKING** Work in pairs. These photos are all from a blog. What do you think the blog is about?

3 **1.16** Read and listen and check your answers.

4 **Read the blog again and answer the questions.**

1 What did Rain's parents do on his first day at high school?
2 How many days did Rain's dad, Dale, wave at the bus?
3 Which other family members got involved?
4 What were the first and last costumes that Dale wore?
5 How much did Dale spend on the costumes?
6 How did he keep the cost so low?
7 What did Rain think about his dad dressing up at the beginning? And at the end?
8 What does Dale plan to do next year?

5 **SPEAKING** Work in pairs and answer the questions.

1 Does Dale sound like a good dad? Explain your reasons.
2 How would you feel if your dad was like Dale? Why?
3 Why do you think Dale wanted to dress up?

D

■ TRAIN TO THiNK ■

Changing your opinions

It can be a mistake to believe something just because it's based on an opinion you've formed. Becoming a critical thinker means continually reflecting on opinions and keeping them only if they are based on evidence that is true.

1   **Which people from the story may have had these opinions at some point? Write their names.**

1   "My dad is the most embarrassing person in the world."   _____

2   "Rain's dad is really silly."   _____

3   "I don't think Dale should do this; it's going to cost a lot of money."   _____

2   **SPEAKING Discuss how the people's opinions in Exercise 1 have changed and why.**

> *Initially, Rain thought that his dad was the most embarrassing dad in the world. But with time, he realized that maybe that wasn't true. He learned to appreciate his dad's sense of humor.*

3   **SPEAKING Think of opinions that you or family members have had and that have changed. Think about music, school, fashion, friends, etc. Discuss in groups.**

An Embarrassing Dad

If you think you have the world's most embarrassing dad, then think again.

American teenager Rain Price has just spent the last year with his dad waving him off to school. OK, so that doesn't sound too bad, but this was no ordinary goodbye because Rain's dad waved goodbye wearing a different costume each day!

It all started on 16-year-old Rain's first day of high school. Like many proud parents, Rochelle and Dale, Rain's mom and dad, stood on their doorstep and waved as Rain went off to school. That evening Rain made the mistake of complaining about how embarrassing that was to him, which gave Dale a great idea.

The next morning as Rain stepped onto the bus outside his house, he could hear all of his classmates laughing at something. He turned around and to his horror, there was his dad waving goodbye, dressed as a football player, complete with football and helmet. But that was just the beginning. For the next 180 school days, rain or shine, Dale waved goodbye to his son dressed in a different costume. One day he was a king waving his sword and shield, the next a chef in his hat and apron, the following a pirate. Then there was Elvis and Wonder Woman. Dale even got other members of the family involved, using Rain's younger brother to play Batman alongside his Robin.

Amazingly Dale only spent $50 on all of his costumes. He got a lot of the costumes from his family's own Halloween collection, and there were several friends and neighbors happy to help.

Some of Rain's friends didn't find it funny, but most of them looked forward to seeing what Dale would be wearing next. Dale also found an international audience for his dressing up, as Rochelle took a daily photo of her husband in costume and put it on their blog, which became a hit on the Internet. Even Rain was eventually able to see the funny side and realized that his dad was pretty cool after all.

But all good things must come to an end, and for the final farewell on the last day of school, Dale dressed up as a pirate and stood next to a sign reading, "It's been fun waving at the bus. Have a great summer." He has no plans to wave Rain off to school next year. Instead, he's looking forward to getting a little more sleep each morning.

GRAMMAR
Quantifiers

1 **Look back at the blog and complete the sentences. Then read the rule and complete the table with *a lot of*, *a little*, *all*, *several*, and *none*.**

1 Like _____ proud parents …

2 He could hear _____ of his classmates laughing at something.

3 He got _____ the costumes from the family's own Halloween collection.

4 There were _____ friends and neighbors happy to help.

5 _____ of Rain's friends didn't find it funny, but _____ of them looked forward to it.

6 He's looking forward to getting _____ more sleep each morning.

RULE: Quantifiers are words and expressions that we use to talk about amount.

0%	1 _____
	hardly any
	a few / 2 _____, not many / much,
	a small number of
	some, 3 _____
	4 _____, lots of, plenty, much /
	many, a good deal of
	most, almost all, the vast majority of
100%	5 _____

---

2 **Choose the correct options.**

1 I've got *a few / a lot of* followers on my blog – more than 200.

2 I spend *a lot of / hardly any* time with my friends – we meet up every day after school and most weekends, too.

3 I spend *most / hardly any* of my time on my tablet. It's the most important thing I have.

4 *A small number / Most* of my teachers are really nice. I really like this school.

5 *Most / All* of my family lives near me, but I have an uncle who lives in Australia.

6 I spend *almost all / hardly any* of my money on downloads. I don't really care about music.

3 **SPEAKING Discuss the sentences in Exercise 2 in pairs. Which of them are true for you?**

Workbook page 28

VOCABULARY
Costumes and uniforms

1 **Look back at the photos of Dale. Which of these things can you see? Write the letters of the photos next to the words. There are two things that aren't in the photos. Check their meaning.**

sword and shield _____   helmet _____

leather jacket _____   cape _____

wig _____   mask _____

belt _____   apron _____

sunglasses _____   football jersey _____

2 **Look at the photos. Who is wearing a costume? Who is wearing a uniform?**

3 **SPEAKING Discuss in pairs.**

1 Do you or does anybody you know wear a uniform? Describe it.

2 What are five jobs in which people wear uniforms?

3 Describe a great costume to wear to a costume party.

Workbook page 30

LISTENING

1 🔊 1.17 **Listen and match the names of the places with the pictures. There is one extra.**

France | Poland | Britain | Japan
Polynesian islands | Argentina

Introduce them early

Keep it in the family

_____   _____

No time for bedtime

Let them solve their own problems

_____   _____

Children only

_____

2 🔊 1.17 **Listen again and choose the correct answers.**

1 Why do many parents feel guilty about the way they bring up their children?
   A They don't give their children enough attention.
   B They feel they are too strict.
   C They don't always do what they think they should do.

2 What did Dr. Keating notice about Argentinian children?
   A They are often more tired.
   B They often sleep too much.
   C They begin developing social skills when they are very young.

3 Why does Dr. Keating feel French children are better eaters?
   A Their parents encourage them to try all sorts of food.
   B They are expected to like all foods from an early age.
   C French cooking is better than British cooking.

4 What surprised Dr. Keating in the Japanese school?
   A The children weren't always well-behaved.
   B The teacher was happy to let the children argue in class.
   C How good the teacher was at helping the children sort out their problems.

5 What does Dr. Keating feel is the most important thing we can learn from *Bringing Up Babies*?
   A Parents in some cultures aren't bringing up their children as well as parents are in others.
   B We can learn a lot about parenting from people in other cultures.
   C Bringing up children isn't easy.

▄ THiNK SELF-ESTEEM ▄

Developing independence

1 Read each sentence and choose a number from 1 to 5 (1 = I strongly agree, 5 = I strongly disagree).

1 Teenagers should set their own bedtimes.   1 2 3 4 5

2 Teenagers should have a part-time job to earn their own spending money.   1 2 3 4 5

3 Teenagers should choose what they eat.   1 2 3 4 5

4 Teenagers should spend weekends with parents / family.   1 2 3 4 5

5 Teenagers should help around the house.   1 2 3 4 5

2 SPEAKING Discuss your answers in small groups. Which question(s) do almost all of you agree on? And which one(s) do almost all of you disagree on? Why?

READING

1 Look at the book cover. What kind of book do you think it is? Read the introduction to find out.

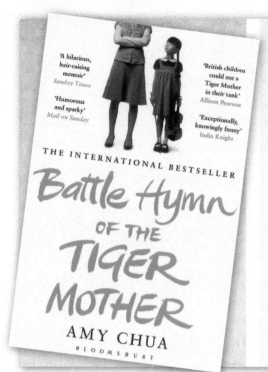

Many people wonder how Chinese parents bring up such successful children. They wonder what Chinese parents do to produce so many mathematical and musical geniuses, what it's like inside the family, and if they could do it, too. Well, Amy Chua can tell them because she's done it.

Her daughters Sophia and Lulu were polite, intelligent, and helpful. They were two years ahead of their classmates in math and had amazing musical abilities. But Sophia and Lulu weren't allowed to have sleepovers, be in a school play, choose what they wanted to do after school, or get any grade lower than an A.

In *Battle Hymn of the Tiger Mother*, Amy Chua tells about her experiences raising her children the "Chinese way." It is a story about a mother and two daughters and two very different cultures. Funny, entertaining, and provocative, this is an important book that will change your ideas about parenting forever.

2 Read these two opinions from readers of Amy Chua's book. Which one is "for" and which one is "against" the tiger mother style of parenting? What reasons do they give?

For and Against – Tiger Moms

This is an interesting book, but Amy Chua's parenting ideas are too strict for me. For example, tiger moms don't let their children watch any TV or play any computer games. How can any child in the 21st century grow up without playing on a computer? What is she trying to do, take away their childhoods?

I do understand that she feels she was only doing the best for her children and trying to help them get ahead in life. But there are lots of kids who spend hours in front of the TV and still do well.

Stephanie, 15

I think Amy Chua's ideas are fantastic. Yes, she was hard on her children at times, but she did raise two amazing children. Her daughters are so confident; they'll definitely do well in life.

Too many parents are too soft on their children these days. They use the TV as a way of keeping them quiet. They don't have enough time for their children. My mom and dad are strict, and they don't let me do a lot of things my friends do. It's hard at times, but they are always there when I need help with my homework or have a problem with other kids at school. They are just trying to do their best for me.

Cesar, 16

3 Read the texts again. Who might say these things? Write Amy Chua, Stephanie, or Cesar.

1 I talk to my parents about my problems. _____
2 No, you can't sleep at Chloe's house. _____
3 Children need to be free to make some of their own decisions. _____
4 My parents don't let me watch much TV, but that's OK. _____
5 You'll thank me one day. _____
6 You can't make kids be what you want them to be. _____

SPEAKING

Work in pairs and answer the questions.

1 Who do you agree with most, Cesar or Stephanie? Why?
2 Can you think of any other examples of rules that strict parents have?

GRAMMAR
so and such (review)

1 **Write the correct words to complete the sentences. Check in the texts. Then complete the rule with *so* and *such*.**

1 Her daughters are _____ confident; they'll do really well in life.

2 Many people wonder how Chinese parents bring up _____ successful children.

> **RULE:** We use *so* and *such* for emphasis.
> [1]_____ (a/an) + (adjective) + noun
> [2]_____ + adjective
>
> We often follow these with a *that* clause to talk about consequences.
> *It was **such a** difficult question **that** I didn't know what to say.*
> *It was **so** hot **that** I couldn't sunbathe.*

2 **Complete with *so* or *such* and then complete the sentences with your own ideas.**

0 It was ___*such*___ a hot day that *we stopped working and went to the beach*.

1 The homework was _____ difficult that …

2 He's _____ a good friend that …

3 The bus was _____ late that …

4 It was _____ an exciting book that …

do and did for emphasis

3 **Complete the sentences from the texts with the missing word. Then read the rule.**

1 I _____ understand that she feels she was only doing the best for her children.

2 She was hard on her children at times, but she _____ raise two amazing children.

> **RULE:** We can use the auxiliaries *do*, *does*, and *did* to add emphasis to what we want to say, often when we're contradicting someone.
> *You didn't like the film, did you? I **did** like the film!*
> *She doesn't want to go to the party. She **does** want to go – she's just shy.*

> **LOOK!** *too* and *(not) enough*
> To say something is more than we need, we use *too*, and to say that it's less, we use *not enough*.
> *too* + adjective
> *too* + *many* + countable noun
> *too* + *much* + uncountable noun
> *not* + adjective + *enough*

4 **Complete the second sentence so it has a similar meaning to the first sentence, using the word in parentheses and *so / such*, *do / did* for emphasis, or *too / (not) enough*. Write between two and five words.**

1 There were too many people at the meeting. Some people had to stand.
There _____ at the meeting, so some people had to stand. (chairs)

2 He spends too much money.
He _____ money. (save)

3 This book isn't interesting enough. I'm not going to finish it.
This book is _____ finish. (boring)

4 You're wrong. I thought the book was really, really good.
I _____ the book. (like)

5 I really think we should leave now.
I _____ stay. (shouldn't)

Workbook page 28

Pronunciation

Adding emphasis with *so*, *such*, *do*, or *did*
Go to page 120.

VOCABULARY
Bringing up children

1 **Complete the text with the words in the list.**

bring | strict | do | soft | childhood
do | get | grow

The toughest job in the world
Most parents want to [1]_____ *their best* for their children and help them [2]_____ *ahead in life*. They try to [3]_____ their children *up* well and give them a happy [4]_____ . But it's not always so easy. Children [5]_____ *up* so fast these days, and it can be difficult to get it right all the time. Of course, parents know the importance of school, and they want their children to [6]_____ *well*, but what happens when the child doesn't want to try? If parents are too [7]_____ , their children might rebel. If they are too [8]_____ , then the children might only do the things they want to do. It's a difficult balancing act and, of course, parents get it wrong sometimes. After all, they're only human, too.

2 **Match the expressions a–h in the text from Exercise 1 with their meanings.**

a make advances in life

b the time of being a child

c get older

d be a success

e have lots of rules

f be as good as you can

g have few (or no) rules

h raise

Workbook page 30

Literature

1 Look at the photo and then read the introduction to the extract. How do you think Marcus feels about his relationship with his mom?

2 🔊 1.20 Read and listen to the extract and check your ideas.

About a Boy by Nick Hornby

Marcus is a schoolboy who lives with his mom, who is depressed. Marcus has a difficult time at school – he gets bullied a lot, especially because of the clothes his mom makes him wear. Marcus has met Will, a rich, lazy man who makes friends with Marcus and buys him new sneakers.

Here, Marcus and his mom are going home after visiting Will at his apartment.

"You're not going round there again," she said on the way home.

Marcus knew she'd say it, and he also knew that he'd take no notice, but he argued anyway.

"Why not?"

"If you've got anything to say, you say it to me. If you want new clothes, I'll get them."

"But you don't know what I need."

"So tell me."

"I don't know what I need. Only Will knows what I need."

"Don't be ridiculous."

"It's true. He knows what things kids wear."

"Kids wear what they put on in the mornings."

"You know what I mean."

"You mean that he thinks he's trendy, and that even though he's […] old he knows which trainers are fashionable, even though he doesn't know the first thing about anything else."

That was exactly what he meant. That was what Will was good at, and Marcus thought he was lucky to have found him.

"We don't need that kind of person. We're doing all right our way."

Marcus looked out of the bus window and thought about whether this was true, and decided it wasn't, that neither of them was doing all right, whichever way you looked at it.

"If you are having trouble it's nothing to do with what shoes you wear, I can tell you that for nothing."

"No, I know, but –"

"Marcus, trust me, OK? I've been your mother for twelve years. I haven't made too bad a job of it. I do think about it. I know what I'm doing."

Marcus had never thought of his mother in that way before, as someone who knew what she was doing. He had never thought that she didn't have a clue either; it was just that what she did with him (for him? to him?) didn't appear to be anything like that. He had always looked on being a mother as straightforward, something like, say, driving: most people could do it, and you could mess it up by doing something really obvious, by driving your car into a bus, or not telling your kid to say please and thank you and sorry (there were loads of kids at school, he reckoned, kids who stole and swore too much and bullied other kids, whose mums and dads had a lot to answer for). If you looked at it that way, there wasn't an awful lot to think about. But his mum seemed to be saying that there was more to it than that. She was telling him she had a plan.

If she had a plan, then he had a choice. He could trust her, believe her when she said she knew what she was doing […] Or he could decide that, actually, she was off her head […] Either way it was scary. He didn't want to put up with things as they were, but the other choice meant he'd have to be his own mother, and how could you be your own mother when you were only twelve? He could tell himself to say please and thank you and sorry, that was easy, but he didn't know where to start with the rest of it. He didn't even know what the rest of it was. He hadn't even known until today that there was a rest of it.

3 Read the extract again. Find the part of the text that tells us that Marcus …

1 is 12 years old.
2 thinks that both he and his mother have problems.
3 begins to see his mother differently.
4 doesn't think very highly of some of the kids at his school.
5 is happy that he has met Will.

4 Match the highlighted words in the extract with the definitions.

1 up-to-date _____
2 do it in a really bad way _____
3 knows nothing at all _____
4 simple; not complicated _____
5 give advice for free _____
6 used bad words _____
7 crazy _____
8 no matter how _____

5 SPEAKING Work in pairs. Discuss the questions.

1 What do you think Marcus means when he talks about "the rest of it" in the last two sentences?
2 Do you think that being a mother or father is straightforward? Why or why not?

WRITING
An essay
Choose one of the titles and write an essay.

- Parents always know best
- Children need rules

Remember:

- write a short introduction to the topic
- give two or three points with examples to support the statement
- give two or three points with examples to argue against the statement
- conclude, giving your opinion

Write your essay in 160–200 words.

FUNCTIONS
Emphasizing

1 Add *so*, *such*, *do*, or *did* to the sentences to make them more emphatic and make any other necessary changes.

1 He's a good father.
2 She gets along well with children.
3 She's patient.
4 My dad tried his best.
5 My parents made some mistakes.
6 She's soft on her children.
7 He's a strict father.
8 Parents get it wrong sometimes.

2 Work in pairs. Who might be talking to whom in each of the sentences in Exercise 1? What was said before? Discuss.

3 Choose one of the sentences and develop it into a six-line dialogue. The sentence you choose from Exercise 1 could appear at the beginning, middle, or end of your dialogue.

_____
_____
_____
_____
_____
_____

4 Think about someone you know who is really good with children or teenagers. Make notes.

Think about:
- their personality
- ways in which they are good with children

5 Work in pairs. Talk about the person. Give examples and use emphasis when you can.

4 THINKING OUTSIDE THE BOX

OBJECTIVES

FUNCTIONS: expressing frustration
GRAMMAR: *used to* vs. *would*; adverbs and adverbial phrases
VOCABULARY: personality adjectives; common adverbial phrases

READING

1 **Look at the photos. Match the photos with these words:**

- [ ] lions
- [ ] cattle
- [ ] a scarecrow
- [ ] a light bulb
- [ ] a battery
- [ ] a solar panel

2 **SPEAKING** Work in pairs or small groups. There are people in a tribe in Africa who want to stop lions from killing their cows. Think of ways they could do this using the items in the photos.

3 **Read the article and match titles A–F with the sections 1–5. There is one extra title.**

- A The lions are finally fooled [ ]
- B A noise scares the lions [ ]
- C No success with scarecrows [ ]
- D The dilemma of the Masai people [ ]
- E The outcomes for animals and the inventor [ ]
- F An idea that didn't quite work [ ]

4 **Read the article again. Seven sentences have been removed. Choose the sentence (A–H) that fits each gap (1–7). There is one extra sentence.**

A In fact, it seemed that the fire actually lit up the cowsheds and made life easier for the lions.

B After a night or two, they got used to seeing this motionless thing and realized it posed no danger.

C Richard's creativity also led to him winning a scholarship at one of the top schools in Kenya.

D The lions stayed far away.

E He connected everything up to some light bulbs that he then put outside the cowshed.

F They went in to kill the cattle.

G Richard, a responsible young man, felt terrible about it and decided he had to do something to keep the lions away without killing them.

H It has also given him the pleasure of seeing people and cattle and lions living together without the conflict that used to exist in the past.

5 **1.21** **Listen and check your answers to Exercise 4. Were your predictions in Exercise 2 right?**

6 **SPEAKING** In pairs or small groups, do the tasks.

1 On a scale of 1–5 agree on how impressive you think Richard's invention is. (1 = not impressive at all, 5 = brilliant!) Say why your group has given this score.

2 Richard gave a talk about his invention. Imagine you were in the audience. Write two questions you would ask him at the end of his talk.

Lion Lights

1 Richard Turere is a member of the Masai tribe from central and eastern Africa. The Masai are traditionally farmers and often keep cattle, an important source of food and income for them. When Richard was a little boy, a big problem for the Masai was that lions would come to their farms and kill their cattle. The lions would often attack at night when it was harder to guard the cattle. The only solution seemed to be to kill the lions. This practice had some degree of success in terms of protecting their cattle, but the Masai weren't very happy about doing this because it was reducing the population of lions.

2 In the Masai tribe, young boys are responsible for protecting their fathers' cattle. Richard Turere used to guard his father's only bull. One day when he was 11, he woke up and found that a lion had killed it. ¹____.

His first idea was to use fire, based on the fact that lions are scared of fire. This plan didn't work at all. ²____. Richard had to come up with something else.

3 His next idea was to use a scarecrow. Richard hoped that he could trick the lions into thinking that there was a person standing guard, but lions are pretty smart. ³____. And then they went in to attack the farm animals.

One night Richard walked around in the cowshed with a flashlight. That night no lions approached the cowshed, so he figured out that they were afraid of the moving light. And being imaginative, he had a new idea.

4 As a bright young man, Richard used to play with things to see how they worked, and he'd learned a lot about electrical gadgets that way. He got a battery and a solar panel to charge it and then he got a signal box from an old motorcycle – the box that makes a light blink to show the direction a driver is turning. ⁴____. The bulbs flashed throughout the night, and the lions thought that someone was walking around inside the cowshed when really everyone was in bed asleep. ⁵____.

5 Since Richard invented his "lion lights," his father has not lost any more cattle to lion attacks. And now Richard's idea is being used in many different places to keep lions, leopards, and elephants away from farms and homes for good. ⁶____. He was also invited to talk at a conference in the U.S. ⁷____.

▮ TRAIN TO THINK ▮

Lateral thinking

1 Read the example.

"Lateral thinking" means solving problems by thinking in a creative way. It means not following the obvious line of thinking. Here is an example.

A woman is driving down a city street at 25 miles per hour. The speed limit is 30 miles per hour. She passes three cars that are traveling at 20 miles per hour. A police officer stops her and gives her a $100 fine. Why?

If we think too much about the speed, we may not get the answer. What does the situation NOT tell us? It doesn't tell us, for example, what time of day it is – so a possible reason for the $100 fine is that it is nighttime, and the woman is driving without her lights on. Or another possible reason for the fine is that the street is one-way, and the woman is driving the wrong way.

2 **SPEAKING** Work in pairs or small groups. Here are more situations. See if you can find possible answers.

1 A father and son are in a bad car crash. They are each taken to different hospitals. The son is taken into the emergency room. The doctor there looks at the boy and says: "That's my son!" *How is this possible?*

2 A woman is lying awake in bed. She dials a number on the phone, says nothing, puts the phone down and then goes to sleep. *Why?*

3 A man lives on the 12th floor of a building. Every morning he takes the elevator down to the entrance and leaves the building. In the evening he gets into the elevator, and, if there is someone else in the elevator, he goes directly to the 12th floor. If the elevator is empty, he goes to the 10th floor and walks up two flights of stairs to his apartment. *Why?*

GRAMMAR
used to vs. would

1 Complete these sentences about the article on page 39 with the words in the list. Then complete the rule by choosing the correct options.

play | attack | exist | guard

1 A conflict used to _____ between the farmers and the lions.

2 The lions would often _____ at night.

3 Richard used to _____ with things to see how they worked.

4 Every night Richard would _____ his father's bull.

> **RULE:** To talk about habits and continuous actions in the past, we can use *used to* or *would*.
> - We use [1]_____ with both action and stative verbs.
> - We only use [2]_____ with action verbs.
> - We use both *would* and *used to* with repeated actions.

2 **Choose the correct option. Sometimes both options are possible.**

1 Manuel *used to / would* live in Oaxaca when he was younger.

2 Elena *used to / would* fix bicycles in her garage every weekend.

3 My sister *used to / would* be afraid of the dark.

4 Every Saturday we *used to / would* play baseball at the park.

5 Holiday dinners with my family *used to / would* last for hours.

6 My cousins *used to / would* join us at the lake in the summer.

3 **Write a question for each answer given.**

0 *Where did you use to go swimming?*
I used to go swimming at the beach.

1 _____
She would finish her homework before dinner.

2 _____
My favorite meal used to be pepperoni pizza.

3 _____
Before I changed to baseball, I used to play soccer.

4 **SPEAKING** Work with a partner. Discuss these things:
- two things that used to be true about you
- two things that you used to do regularly

Workbook page 36

VOCABULARY
Personality adjectives

1 Which of the adjectives in the list are used in the article to describe Richard Turere? What do they mean?

~~bad-tempered~~ | responsible | decisive | bright imaginative | organized | impatient | practical confident | cautious | arrogant | dull

2 **Complete the spaces with a word from Exercise 1.**

0 Roberto gets angry all the time, and he complains a lot. He's pretty *bad-tempered* .

1 Barbara understands things quickly. She's very _____.

2 Carmen doesn't like taking risks. She's a very _____ person.

3 Dana's great because she makes her mind up really quickly – a really _____ girl.

4 Raul never has anything interesting to say – he's so _____!

5 Eva always has wonderful ideas; she's very _____.

6 Ian wants everything, and he wants it now! He's pretty _____.

7 Oscar always knows where things are and what he has to do – he's very _____.

8 Rita is someone you can trust with difficult jobs. She's _____.

3 **SPEAKING** Work with a partner. Use the adjectives in Exercises 1 and 2 to describe yourself, a best friend, and someone in your family.

Workbook page 38

SPEAKING

1 Work in pairs. Think of five different people and write sentences to describe them, but don't use the adjective.

> *Jo is waiting for her friend who's two minutes late. She calls her to see where she is.*

2 Change partners and read your sentences. Can they guess the adjective you were thinking of?

> *Jo is impatient.*

3 Ask your partner extra questions about the adjective.

> *Do you often get impatient in this kind of situation?*

LISTENING
Being imaginative

1 **Work alone. Look at the two tasks. Think of ideas for both. Then compare with a partner.**

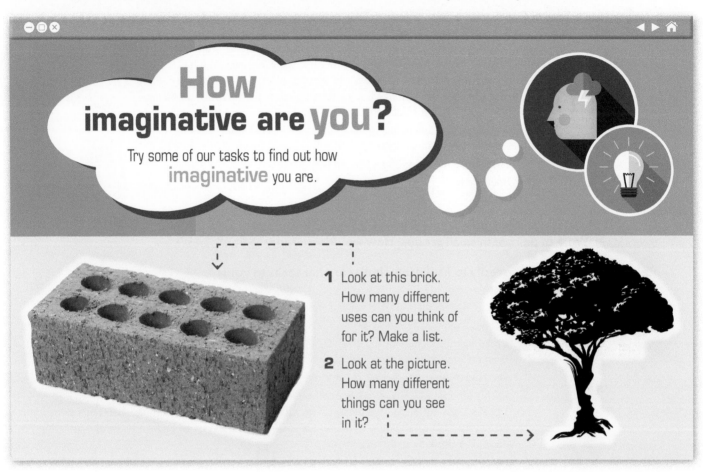

How imaginative are you?

Try some of our tasks to find out how **imaginative** you are.

1 Look at this brick. How many different uses can you think of for it? Make a list.

2 Look at the picture. How many different things can you see in it?

2 🔊 1.22 **Rosa and Mark did the tasks. Listen to their conversation and complete the tasks.**

1 Note the six uses Rosa thought of for the brick.

_____

2 Note the four things Mark saw in the picture.

_____

3 **SPEAKING** **In groups, compare Rosa's and Mark's ideas with what you thought of in Exercise 1.**

4 🔊 1.22 **Listen again and complete each** ✳ **sentence with no more than three words.**

1 Rosa only _____ six ideas.

2 Rosa thinks you can put the brick on top of a _____ so that they don't blow away.

3 Mark thinks Rosa is wrong about using the brick as a hammer to put _____ into a wall.

4 Rosa doesn't understand how Mark can see a _____ in the picture.

5 Mark says the quiz is meant to demonstrate _____ people are.

6 Rosa says that Mark shouldn't be _____ on himself.

▮ THiNK VALUES ▮
Appreciating creative solutions

1 **Choose the best way to finish this sentence.**

I think the activities in Exercise 1 tell us that …

1 it's important to be imaginative. ☐

2 being imaginative is better than being practical. ☐

3 you can be an imaginative person even if you're not good at these activities. ☐

4 some people are not as imaginative as others. ☐

5 everybody's imagination is different. ☐

2 **Now put these in order of importance for you. (1 = most important, 5 = least important)**

☐ being practical
☐ being imaginative
☐ knowing a lot of things
☐ being responsible
☐ being organized

3 **SPEAKING** **Work in pairs. Compare your answers in Exercises 1 and 2. How similar are your ideas?**

READING

1 Read the post from Paul on the Answers4U website. What problem does he have?

Hello everyone,

I'm 18 and I'm going to start college soon. I'm going to study journalism because I want to work in TV. In the first semester everyone has to take a class called *Creative Thinking and Writing*. At first I thought it would be easy. But now I'm scared I'll only get through it with a lot of problems because I'm not a creative person at all!

I'm scared that I'm going to look foolish and that I won't pass the class. I'm not sure I can go through with this.

Can anyone help me? Some tips on being creative would be good!

Thanks a lot!

Paul

2 **SPEAKING** Work in pairs or in small groups. How would you reply to Paul's post?

3 Read what Sarah writes in reply to Paul. How similar are her ideas to yours?

Hi Paul,

I read your post, and I can completely relate to it. I've been in exactly the same situation – I even majored in journalism just like you. So here are my thoughts.

The first thing to say is that if the class is any good, it'll help you with your problem! But I can totally understand why you're anxious.

You say, "I'm not a creative person." But that's not true – everyone's creative! Don't deny your creativity. If you tell yourself you're not creative, you'll start to believe it. So the first thing to do is stop thinking like that!

People sometimes talk about "thinking outside the box" – you know, thinking in a different way – but actually, the only "box" is the way we've been brought up to see problems. A central obstacle to our ability to think creatively is the assumption that there must always be a "right" answer to every question or problem, and that limits creative thinking. So, try to stop seeing things as "right" or "wrong."

Another problem is this: We come up with an idea and then we immediately think, "Oh, that's no good." People criticize their own thoughts and ideas before they give them a chance to grow! While you're thinking, just try to brainstorm ideas in an enjoyable way – then choose the best ideas later.

And don't worry about looking foolish. If you try an idea and other people laugh at it, that's their problem, not yours. Try to look at the class as a way to have fun and learn something new. Work hard, don't hold yourself back, do everything with enthusiasm, and you'll be fine.

Anyway, enough from me. I hope these ideas help.

Sarah

4 Read the letters again. Mark the statements T (true) or F (false).

1 Paul intends to become a newspaper reporter.
2 Paul thinks he is going to fail his class.
3 Paul wants advice about how to be creative.
4 Sarah thinks the class itself should help Paul with his problem.
5 Sarah can see why Paul is worried.
6 Sarah believes that it is a bad thing to say you're not creative.
7 Sarah thinks that problems have correct solutions.
8 Sarah thinks people shouldn't criticize their own ideas.

5 **SPEAKING** Work with a partner. Discuss the questions.

1 Do you think Sarah's answer is useful? Why or why not?
2 Which of her comments do you like the most? The least?

Pronunciation

Pronouncing words with *gh*

Go to page 120.

GRAMMAR
Adverbs and adverbial phrases

1   **For each sentence, put a letter in the box to say if the underlined adverb relates to time (T), manner (M), place (P), or certainty (C).**

0   I read your post and can <u>completely</u> relate to it.   `M`

1   I read about it <u>recently</u>.

2   This is <u>definitely</u> the best album they've ever made.

3   You can buy most of the things you need <u>locally</u>.

4   You are capable of thinking <u>creatively</u>.

5   We got <u>home</u> at nine o'clock.

6   This is <u>possibly</u> the best work I've ever done.

7   You can choose the best ideas <u>later</u>.

8   I applied for the job, and, <u>surprisingly</u>, I got it!

2   **Look back at Sarah's reply on page 42. What verbs do these words qualify?**

1   completely   3   creatively   5   hard

2   totally   4   immediately

3   **Sometimes we use adverbial phrases instead of an adverb. Add the words below to lists A and B. Then choose the correct words to complete the rule.**

interesting | friendly | fear | surprise | enthusiasm | strange

A	B
in an enjoyable way	with / without difficulty
in a horrible way	with / without excitement
in a different way	with / without interest
in a _____ way	with / without _____
in an _____ way	with / without _____
in a _____ way	with / without _____

> **RULE:** We often form adverbial phrases with:
> * in a/an + [1]noun / adjective way
> * with/without + [2]noun / adjective

4   **Complete the sentences. Use expressions from Exercise 3. There might be more than one possibility.**

0   I really like football, so I went to the game with
     interest / enthusiasm / excitement .

1   The first time I met him, he looked at me in
     _____.

2   The homework was easy – I did it without
     _____.

3   Some of the people at the party were dressed in
     _____.

4   It was a great show, and I watched it with
     _____.

5   I don't really like parties, so I went to Gabi's without
     _____.

Workbook page 37

VOCABULARY
Common adverbial phrases

1   **Use the words from the list to complete the definitions.**

~~in secret~~ | in a row | on purpose
in a panic | by accident | in a hurry
in private | in public

If you do something …

0   without other people knowing, you do it
     in secret .

1   that other people can hear or see, you do
     it _____.

2   that other people can't hear or see, you do
     it _____.

3   that you intended to do, you do it
     _____.

4   that you didn't intend to do, you do it
     _____.

5   while afraid and without thinking properly,
     you do it _____.

6   quickly, you do it _____.

7   three times without a break, you do it three
     times _____.

2   **Choose the correct options to complete the sentences.**

1   The two of us went into a room, alone, so
     that we could talk *in a hurry / in private*.

2   He broke my phone, and I'm really angry.
     I'm sure he did it *on purpose / in a panic*.

3   I woke up late four days *in a row /
     by accident*!

4   I was very late, so I had to leave the house
     on purpose / in a hurry.

5   He was *in secret / in a panic* because he
     couldn't find his phone.

6   I'm so sorry that I lost your notebook. I left
     it on the bus *on purpose / by accident*.

7   She did it late at night *in secret / in a panic*.
     No one knew anything.

3   **SPEAKING Work with a partner. Discuss the questions.**

1   When were you last in a hurry?

2   What can you do five times in a row?

3   Give an example of something you did on
     purpose and wish you hadn't.

4   Give an example of something you got right
     by accident.

5   When and why was the last time you were
     in a panic?

Workbook page 38

Writer's block

1 Look at the photos and answer the questions.

1 Look at what the teacher has written on the board. What do you think the homework is?

2 How does Emma feel about the homework?

3 Do you think Justin is being helpful?

2 ◀)) 1.25 Now read and listen to the photostory. Check your ideas.

TEACHER OK, everyone, so this is your assignment, and it's due Friday – a short story of 500 words.

EMMA Five hundred words? She can't be serious!

TEACHER And the story has to end with the words, "Thanks, you saved my life!"

EMMA What? This is awful. I can't do that. I'm hopeless at creative writing.

TEACHER It has to be original, though. No using old stories and changing them a little here and there. I want something that's yours and yours alone. Be creative! OK, class dismissed. See you Friday.

EMMA And she wants it by Friday! That's the day after tomorrow. I'll never come up with anything that fast. An original story? No way.

LIAM Sounds like you've already given up.

NICOLE Liam's right. I mean, come on, it can't be that hard, can it?

EMMA An original story, 500 words long? I think that's pretty hard.

JUSTIN What's the ending again?

EMMA Someone says, "Thanks, you saved my life!"

JUSTIN OK, that's five words. So far, so good. All you need is another 495.

EMMA You know what, Justin? I may not be very good at creative writing, but I can think of a few words for you right now!

NICOLE OK, calm down.

JUSTIN Well, I'm sorry, Emma, but all you have to do is think of some story you've read or a movie you've seen …

EMMA No, no, that's just it. It has to be original.

LIAM But how would she know if it wasn't original?

EMMA You don't know Ms. Jenkins. She's read every book, seen every movie.

JUSTIN I know! Why don't you write a story about a girl who has to write a story, and her friends give her a great idea, and then she says, "Thanks, you saved my life!" The hero could be a really cool dude named Justin.

NICOLE Give it a rest, Justin!

EMMA OK, well, this isn't getting me anywhere. I'm out of here. See you guys later. And thanks for all the help, Justin. I really appreciate it.

JUSTIN What did I do?

LIAM Well, you were kind of a jerk, Justin. You can see that Emma's stressed out already, and you weren't exactly helpful.

DEVELOPING SPEAKING

3 Work in pairs. Discuss what happens next in the story. Write down your ideas.

We think Emma watches a movie and gets an idea.

4 ▶️ **EP2** Watch to find out how the story continues.

5 Match the sentence beginnings and endings.

1 Emma sees a woman who
2 The woman works for
3 The woman is desperate because
4 Emma tries to help
5 When Emma gets an idea
6 Emma gets the keys out
7 Emma's really happy about

a but she can't get the keys out.
b the last thing the woman says.
c has dropped her keys.
d using something she got at a dry cleaner's.
e an art gallery.
f she goes to a store nearby.
g she doesn't have a spare set of keys.

PHRASES FOR FLUENCY

1 Find these expressions in the photostory. Who says them? How do you say them in your language?

1 (She) can't be serious! _____
2 (What's the ending) again? _____
3 Calm down. _____
4 That's just it. _____
5 Give it a rest. _____
6 (I'm) out of here. _____

2 Use the expressions in Exercise 1 to complete the sentences.

1 I know you told me before, but what's your name _____ ?

2 A Let's go for a walk in the park.
  B A walk in the park? You _____ ! It's raining!

3 A Come on, we're late!
  B _____ , we're not late. We've got 15 minutes.

4 A Your hair looks really weird!
  B Oh, _____ , Michelle. I'm tired of you criticizing me all the time. I'm _____ .

5 A Let's go to the mall or out to dinner or something.
  B I don't feel like going out tonight.
  A _____ . You never want to go out!

WordWise
good

1 Use the phrases in the list to complete these sentences from the unit so far.

~~for good~~ | So far, so good. | not very good at
It's no good | It's a good thing | it's all good

0 The lights have stopped animals from coming to the farm *for good* .
1 I'm _____ creative thinking.
2 That's five words. _____ .
3 I never liked that dress anyway. So _____ .
4 _____ . I can't get the keys out.
5 _____ I'm such a reliable person.

2 Which phrase means:

1 forever
2 It's not successful.
3 Everything is all right.
4 not talented at
5 We have started but not finished, but everything has been OK until now.
6 I'm/We're/You're lucky that …

Workbook page 38

FUNCTIONS
Expressing frustration

1 Read the photostory again. Which of these things does Emma not say? What do all the sentences have in common?

1 I can't (do that).
2 I'm hopeless (at …)
3 This is hopeless!
4 No chance!
5 I give up.
6 I'll never (come up with anything).
7 This is pointless.

2 Think about the woman who loses her keys. Write three things she might have thought using the expressions in Exercise 1.

I'll never get the keys out!

WRITING
A story

Write a story. The story must end with the words:

"Thanks, you saved my life!"
Write between 120–150 words.

∎ THiNK EXAMS ∎

LISTENING
Part 3: Multiple matching

Workbook page 35

1   🔊 1.26 **You will hear five different people talking about an after-school art group. Choose from the list (A–H) what each speaker likes most about the group. Use the letters only once. There are three extra letters that you do not need to use.**

A   It's fun to learn different techniques.

B   It's good to meet people with the same interest.

C   It's fun to spend more time with your friends.

D   It will be useful for the future.

E   It's interesting to find out about painters from other times.

F   The teacher really helps you achieve good results.

G   Being into art is cool.

H   It brings out your creative side.

Speaker 1 ☐
Speaker 2 ☐
Speaker 3 ☐
Speaker 4 ☐
Speaker 5 ☐

WRITING
Part 2: An email

Workbook page 43

2   You have recently asked about attending an art camp for a week. You have received the following reply.

⊖ ⊡ ⊗   ◄ ► ⌂

Thank you for your email. It sounds like you would be perfect for the camp. We offer lessons in all types of art. However, if you could let us know which area you are most interested in and why, we can make sure we won't disappoint you.

It would also be helpful to know if there is any food you don't eat. This will make life easier for our cook.

Looking forward to your reply.

Sincerely,

Hillary Mason

Write your reply to Hillary in 140–190 words in an appropriate style.

TEST YOURSELF

VOCABULARY

1 Complete the sentences with the words in the list. There are four extra words.

best | public | strict | grow | organized | well | worst | bad-tempered
panic | soft | helmets | secret | row | imaginative

1 My parents were really _____ when I was young. I couldn't do everything I wanted to do.
2 My mother was very _____. The house was always tidy – everything in the right place.
3 She always had our school things ready for us, even our bike _____.
4 My brothers and I were often very difficult. I don't think she was ever _____.
5 Both my parents did everything they could to help us do _____ in life.
6 They kept any arguments for when they were alone. They never argued in _____.
7 My dad invented great games for us. He really was very _____.
8 He was very calm. I never saw him in a _____.
9 Once we helped him prepare a surprise party for my mom. Everything had to be done in _____ so she wouldn't find out.
10 I think we were lucky to _____ up in such a nice family.

/10

GRAMMAR

2 Complete the sentences with the words in the list. There are two extra words.

few | enthusiasm | little | travel | most | live | none | surprise

1 Josh doesn't like boxing, so he went to the boxing match without much _____.
2 _____ of my friends could come to the party; they were all on vacation.
3 When I was a child, I used to _____ in Mexico City.
4 Luis has seen lots of movies, but he's only read a _____ books.
5 Patricia loved visiting her grandparents. She would _____ to see them all the time.
6 Samya wanted to spend a _____ more time on the photo selection for the project.

3 Find and correct the mistake in each sentence.

1 The test was such difficult that nobody got everything right.
2 Harry use to be alone a lot when he was younger.
3 Sara would to be scared of the dark.
4 Martin listened with interesting to the interview with the local politician.
5 There was hardly any of space on the shelf, so I couldn't put the books there.
6 My grandmother always preferred her laptop. She never would to use a tablet.

/12

FUNCTIONAL LANGUAGE

4 Choose the correct options.

1 A I'll *never / give up* write a poem.
   B Don't be *so / such* pessimistic! I'm sure you can do it.
2 A But you're *so / such* a good writer. Can't you write one for me?
   B No *chance / I can't* do that – but I'll help.
3 A Oh, dear! This project is *so / such* difficult.
   B What's the problem? You're usually *so / such* an imaginative person.
4 A Oh! I'm *give up / hopeless* at drawing. This dog looks more like a bear!
   B Come on! Don't get *so / such* angry! Why don't you find a dog on the Internet and copy it?

/8

MY SCORE **/30**

| 22 – 30 |
| 10 – 21 |
| 0 – 9 |

5 | SCREEN TIME

OBJECTIVES

FUNCTIONS: advice and obligation
GRAMMAR: obligation, permission, and prohibition (review); necessity: *didn't have to / didn't need to / needn't have*; ability in the past: (*could, was/were able to, managed to, succeeded in*)
VOCABULARY: technology (nouns); technology (verbs)

READING

1 How many different types of screens can you see in the photos? Can you think of other types of screens that you see or use in a typical day? Make a list.

2 Thinking of the list you made in Exercise 1, what are the advantages and disadvantages of having so many different screens in your daily life?

3 🔊 1.27 Read and listen to the articles and find out which of your ideas from Exercise 2 are mentioned.

4 Read the articles again. Match them with the titles. There is one extra title.

A The consequences of 24-hour availability ☐
B It's a rich person's world ☐
C Parents need to establish limits ☐
D Fewer screens, better lives ☐

5 Which article talks about …

a the harm screens can do even when we're not watching them?
b why none of us are really out of contact anymore?
c the effect of screen time on the family?
d how it's almost impossible to live without modern technology?
e the financial implications of trying to limit the use of technology?
f the effects of spending too much time in front of a screen?

6 **SPEAKING** Work in pairs. Discuss the questions.

1 Think of a screen that your parents complain about you using too much. Why do they complain?

2 Think of one type of screen that you couldn't live without and one you could live without. Tell your partner and give reasons.

SMART SCREENS?

1 *How much screen time do you let your children have? This has become one of the most challenging issues of modern parenting. Most experts agree that screen time should be limited and warn against allowing children to spend too long in front of one; however, it's not always easy to follow their advice. Clearly children can't see the potential harm that an excessive amount of time spent in front of a screen might do. Furthermore, peer pressure means that they feel unfairly treated when their parents say that they have to turn off their electronic devices, which can lead to stressful family situations. It's easy to see why so many parents give in and let their children stare at screens for far too long. Unfortunately, doing so creates greater problems in the long run, including negative effects on attention span, fitness levels, and mood, as children become more irritable after spending a lot of time watching screens. Of course, this is a situation that has been around since TV viewing became a common habit in the 1960s. With the predominance of screens in modern life, however, it's become a lot more serious.*

2 People sleep better in darkness, but is darkness even possible these days? Far from being dark at night, most modern cities are now awash with color from artificial lights. Huge TV screens and neon signs are making it difficult for many residents to get a good night's sleep. One city has decided to take action against this new form of pollution.

With a population of over 11 million, São Paulo is the biggest city in Brazil and one of the ten biggest cities in the world. Not long ago, the city government passed the "Clean City Law," which stated that large outdoor advertising was no longer allowed. All existing signs had to be taken down despite the financial losses it might mean. Advertising companies were not happy, but the people living in the city were. More than 70 percent of residents agreed that the ban had improved their quality of life.

3 Cell phones have become such an important part of our lives that it's difficult to imagine how we could live without them. Of course, making and receiving calls is only one of their functions. We use them to take photos, record videos, check email and Facebook, surf the Internet, get directions, play games, shop, check in for a flight – the list seems endless. It wasn't all that long ago, however, that people didn't need cell phones. We managed to live without them quite easily, and maybe we were all just a little bit happier. In the old days, if you wanted to reach someone, you called their house. If they weren't home, that was just too bad. But mobile phones are, well, mobile. We now call the person directly, and if they don't answer immediately, we get annoyed. We have gotten used to being able to reach people all day every day. The result of this expectation is that no one is allowed to relax anymore. We're expected to be reachable whether we're at work, at home, on vacation, or even asleep. Have we lost the ability to disconnect from others and truly relax?

■ TRAIN TO THINK

The PMI strategy

A good brainstorming strategy you can use when making decisions is the PMI strategy. On a piece of paper, draw three columns and head them "plus," "minus," and "interesting." Write down the positive consequences (plus) and negative consequences (minus) of the decision and also what would be "interesting" about carrying it out.

1 Look at the example below. Can you add any more ideas to the columns?

Books should be banned from schools

plus	minus	interesting
Lessons would be more interactive. Students wouldn't have to carry heavy books to and from school.	Students would spend even more time looking at screens.	How would this change teachers' lives?

2 SPEAKING Work in groups. Choose one of the situations. Use the PMI strategy to come to a decision.

- Your school has been asked to put on a play, but you and your friends are not sure if you should take part since it will mean staying after school for the next six weeks.

- Your group has been asked to take part in a reality TV show. It involves living without any technology for a month. You are not sure whether you should take part.

- Your group has been invited to make a recommendation to the public transportation agency of your town about whether cell phones should be forbidden on buses, trains, and subways.

GRAMMAR
Obligation, permission, and prohibition (review)

1 **Complete the sentences about the articles on page 49. Then complete the rule with** *let, must, should, need to,* **and** *not be allowed to.*

1 Most experts agree that screen time _____ be limited.

2 They feel unfairly treated when their parents say they _____ turn off their electronic devices.

3 Many parents give in and _____ their children stare at screens all the time.

> **RULE:** To express obligation or necessity, we can use *have to* or [1]_____ (as in sentence 2).
> To say something is (or isn't) a good idea, we can use [2]_____ (as in sentence 1).
> To express no obligation or necessity, we can use *don't have to* or *don't* [3]_____ .
> To express permission, we can use [4]_____ (as in sentence 3) and to say that something is not permitted we use [5]_____ .

> **LOOK!**
> - *had better* = something is a good idea and is often used as a warning. The form is always *had better* + base form of verb, even when talking about the present.
> - *be supposed to* = there's an obligation to do something, but in reality people don't always do it. It is always used in the passive form (like *be allowed to*).

2 **Complete the second sentence so that it has a similar meaning to the first sentence. Use the given word. You must use between two and five words including the given word.**

1 Their daughter can't go out after 8 p.m. (allowed)
Their daughter _____ go out after 8 p.m.

2 Our teacher expects us to raise our hands if we want to ask a question. (supposed)
We _____ raise our hands if we want to ask a question.

3 Their son isn't allowed to watch TV all day. (let)
They _____ their son watch TV all day.

4 You should really turn off the TV if you don't want to get a headache. (better)
You _____ off the TV if you don't want to get a headache.

> Workbook page 46

FUNCTIONS
Advice and obligation

1 **Imagine an exchange student is coming to your school for a few weeks. Write down three rules and three pieces of advice to help them.**

> *You have to arrive at school by 9 a.m.*

2 **SPEAKING Compare your sentences in pairs.**

VOCABULARY
Technology (nouns)

1 **Match the words with the pictures.**
1 USB port | 2 headphones | 3 adaptor
4 webcam | 5 plug | 6 charger | 7 "at" symbol
8 power cord | 9 case | 10 wireless router

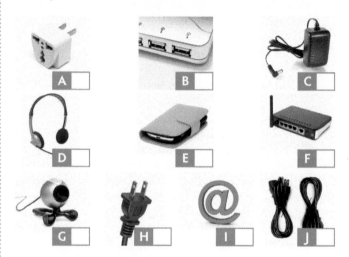

2 **Complete the sentences using the words in Exercise 1.**

1 There's something wrong with that email address. There's no _____ in it.

2 I forgot to bring a U.K. _____ , so I couldn't plug in my laptop.

3 I left the _____ for my phone at home, and I'm almost out of battery. Can I borrow yours?

4 You can't get a Wi-Fi signal? Have you checked if the _____ is on?

5 My laptop's only got one _____ so I can't plug in my mouse and my phone at the same time.

6 I dropped my phone yesterday, and it broke. I think I should get a _____ for my new one.

7 I couldn't use my laptop. I left the _____ at home and my battery's dead.

8 I'm going to plug in my _____ . I don't want everyone to hear what you're saying.

9 It's the wrong kind of _____ . You need an adaptor.

10 Turn on your _____ . I'd like to see your new place.

> Workbook page 48

LISTENING

1 **SPEAKING** Mark the statements with 1 (agree), 2 (depends), or 3 (disagree). Then compare your findings in class.

Watching TV …

1 can damage your brain.

2 is bad for your education.

3 is addictive.

4 is expensive.

5 is not as satisfying as spending time with friends.

2 🔊 1.28 Listen to the conversation. Which of the statements in Exercise 1 does Juana mention? _____

3 🔊 1.28 Listen again. Complete the sentences.

1 Juana wants to know why Mateo missed _____ on Saturday.

2 Mateo's been spending a lot of time _____ stuff on his tablet recently.

3 Mateo asks Juana if she thinks he's becoming a _____ .

4 Mateo's been staying up until _____ recently.

5 Juana warns Mateo about hidden advertising or product _____ in movies.

6 Mateo wants to invite Juana to an outdoor _____ on Saturday.

GRAMMAR

Necessity: *didn't have to / didn't need to / needn't have*

1 Look at the examples from the listening and answer the questions. Then complete the rule with *didn't have to / didn't need to do / needn't have done*.

I didn't need to go [to the stadium] because I was able to watch it live online.
You didn't have to buy the tickets! I mean, you needn't have done that.

1 Did Mateo go to the stadium?

2 Did Mateo buy two tickets?

> **RULE:** When we use [1]_____, it means that someone did something, but in fact it wasn't necessary.
>
> When we use [2]_____, it often means that someone didn't do something because it wasn't necessary.
>
> [3]_____ can have either meaning.

2 Match the sentences 1–6 with the correct meaning, a or b.

1 Mom cooked a big meal for us, but we'd already eaten.

2 Mom came and ate with us at the restaurant.

  a She needn't have cooked.

  b She didn't need to cook.

3 I spent forever on my homework last night, and now Mr. Peters isn't here to take it.

4 Mr. Peters told us we could choose to do this assignment or not.

  a I didn't need to do it.

  b I needn't have done it.

5 She took her umbrella, but it was a really sunny day.

6 The forecast said that it was going to be a sunny day, so she left her umbrella at home.

  a She didn't need to take it.

  b She needn't have taken it.

Workbook page 47

VOCABULARY

Technology (verbs)

Rewrite the sentences, replacing the words in italics with the phrases in the list in the correct form.

to upgrade (your system) | to stream (a video)
to save (a document) | to browse the Internet
to plug (a laptop) in | to sync devices
to post an update

1 Jack's watching yesterday's game. He's *watching it on the Internet without downloading* it.

2 **A** What are you looking for?

  B Nothing really. I'm just *looking at various websites*.

3 I think you should spend some money *on improving* your operating system; it's very old.

4 You should always *make sure different devices (laptop, tablet, etc.) contain the same information* so you've always got a backup.

5 **A** The printer isn't working.

  B Well, that's no surprise. It isn't *connected to the electricity supply*.

6 Mia hasn't *added new content to her blog* for a week. I hope she's OK.

7 My friend is always losing files because he forgets to *store information on an electronic device* regularly.

Workbook page 48

SPEAKING

Discuss in pairs.

1 How often do you post updates on social media?

2 Which devices do you sync?

3 What was the last TV show you streamed?

> **Pronunciation**
>
> The /ə/ sound
> Go to page 120. 🔊

READING

1 **Look at the photo and answer the questions.**

   1 What do you think the relationship between the people is?

   2 What do you think they are doing?

2 **Read through the article quickly and check your answers.**

3 **Read again. Find examples in the article of how elderly people used technology.**

Great success for teenage teachers: When silver surfers get connected

A new documentary called *Silver Surfers* shows the inspiring story of a group of teens helping elderly people improve the quality of their lives by teaching them how to make use of the Internet. The people were between 76 and 93 years old.

Rosemary Raynes, the director of the documentary, got the idea for the film when talking to her sisters, Molly and Kayly, about a project they had started several years before in Kingston, Ontario, Canada. The two teenagers and a group of friends had a clear goal: they wanted to help elderly people feel more connected to others with the help of the Internet.

The two sisters started their project after witnessing how the Internet had changed their own grandparents' lives. Their grandparents could use the Internet at a basic level but wanted to become more proficient. After the girls had given them a few basic lessons, they were able to use the computer confidently and became enthusiastic users of Skype, Facebook, and email.

Molly and Kayly were so motivated by that success that they got several of their friends to join them. Together, they started to visit a local senior center. Many of the people there couldn't even turn on a computer without help, but the young people were amazed how much they had learned after only a few lessons.

The teen teachers quickly realized that the cyber seniors all had very different interests. Some of them wanted to use Facebook to stay in touch with family members, some of whom had immigrated to countries as far away as Australia. Others wanted to get ideas for traveling, learn how to play an instrument, or find some new and different recipes.

The results of the project were amazing: 89-year-old Sheila, along with a friend, managed to create a YouTube cooking tutorial; 93-year-old Marilyn succeeded in making a rap video; Albert, 89, initially wanted to learn how to use the Web to find friends he fought with in World War II, and in doing so, he was struck by how easy it was to reconnect online with people he hadn't seen in decades. He even managed to use his newly acquired skills to reunite with his daughter, who he had lost touch with years before.

Silver Surfers has been met with great enthusiasm in several countries, and a number of follow-up projects have been launched. They are all aimed at helping elderly people. The seniors they have worked with can now explore the benefits of technology and stay in touch with others – all thanks to a wonderful initiative by two teenage girls.

4 **Read again and answer the questions in your notebook.**

   1 What is Silver Surfers?

   2 What does it show?

   3 Who started the project?

   4 What inspired them to start the project?

   5 Who did they get to join them?

   6 Where did they start giving lessons?

   7 What were some of the elderly people's interests?

   8 What were some of their achievements?

5 **SPEAKING** **Discuss with a partner.**

   1 What do you think of the Silver Surfer Project?

   2 Would you be prepared to join such a project? Why or why not?

   3 Which example of the seniors' achievements impresses you the most?

   4 Have you ever tried to help someone you know with technology? Did you manage to teach them successfully?

GRAMMAR

Ability in the past: *could, was/were able to, managed to, succeeded in*

1 Read the examples from the article and then complete the rule with *managed, succeeded, could, couldn't*.

1 Many of the people there **couldn't** even switch on a computer without help.

2 After [...] a few basic IT lessons, they **were able to** use the computer confidently.

3 The outcomes of the project were amazing: 89-year-old Sheila [...] **managed to** create a YouTube cooking tutorial.

4 93-year-old Marilyn **succeeded in** making a rap video.

> **RULE:** To talk about ability generally in the past we use [1]_____ / couldn't.
>
> To talk about ability at specific moments in the past, we use *was / were able to* ([2]_____ *to* + infinitive, or [3]_____ *in* + gerund).
>
> To talk about a lack of ability at specific moments in the past, we use [4]_____ / *wasn't (weren't) able to*.

2 Choose the correct answer to complete the sentences.

1 She broke her cell phone a week ago. She _____ to access any social networks since then.
A couldn't B hasn't been able C hasn't succeeded

2 He was so moved by the award he received that he _____ continue with his speech.
A could B wasn't able to C succeeded in

3 He played football again for the first time after his injury, but he only _____ play for 20 minutes.
A could B succeeded in C managed to

4 She had to ask several people until she finally _____ in finding some help.
A managed B succeeded C could

5 My little brother _____ to walk just before his first birthday.
A could B was able C succeeded

6 I tried to climb that mountain once, but I _____ to get to the top because of the bad weather.
A couldn't B didn't succeed C didn't manage

Workbook page 47

■ THiNK SELF-ESTEEM ■

Learning from elderly people

1 You're going to talk about an elderly person who has qualities that you admire. Make notes on why you admire this person.

2 Which of the qualities that you noted do you think you would like to have in your own life?

3 What could you do to develop those qualities?

4 SPEAKING Discuss your ideas with your partner.

5 Write a paragraph that summarizes what you have learned by thinking about the person.

One of our neighbors is a man named Mr. Carter. He is over 80 years old, but in many ways he seems very young. He has an excellent sense of humor, and I've had great conversations with him. He's a very good listener and asks very interesting questions. If there is one thing I would like to learn from him for my own life, it's the way he sets goals for himself and goes for them. For example, Mr. Carter has a little swimming pool in his backyard, and he goes for a swim every day, no matter what the weather is like. And the weather can get really cold where we live!

Culture

1 **SPEAKING** Discuss the questions in pairs.

1 Have you ever seen a silent movie?

2 Have you ever seen a movie in black and white?

2 Scan the text to find the answers to these questions.

1 What technology did Etienne Gaspar Robert use to impress his audiences?

2 What did Edison and Dickenson invent, and how did it work?

3 What years are referred to as the "Golden Era of Hollywood"?

3 🔊 1.31 Read and listen to the article. Check your answers.

When pictures learned to walk and talk: The history of film

Early days: the magic lantern

Since its early days, the evolution of the art of film has been influenced by the development of science.

Several scientists in the 18th century (among them Kircher, Huygens, and Fontana) developed devices that used hand-drawn pictures on a reflecting surface, a candle, and a simple lens to project images onto a wall. These devices are what are now referred to as "magic lanterns."

More than a hundred years later, in 1798 in Paris, Etienne Gaspar Robert's magic lantern presentations were the talk of the town. His audience sat on one side of a transparent screen while he sat on the other with his magic lantern. He regularly succeeded in scaring his enthusiastic audiences with images of witches,

ghosts, and other spooky creatures. He created these images by using various technical tricks such as moving the lantern, using a shutter to create fading effects, and changing the focus. In many ways, his shows were the forerunner of modern horror films.

The invention of film

The late 19th century saw the development of reel film. At first it was made of paper and then, later, of another scientific invention called celluloid. In the U.S., Thomas Edison and William Dickenson invented a camera that automatically took a picture of a moving object every half second. The pictures were then transferred onto film and could be watched through a machine called the Kinetoscope. The film could only be watched by one person at a time looking through a small window to see the moving images.

The next step in the evolution of film was when Auguste and Louis Lumière developed the *cinematographe*, which made it possible to take moving pictures and project large images. This used the same lens technology as that developed for the magic lantern. They started producing short films that were all roughly 50 seconds long. The most famous one was *The Arrival of a Train*

at La Ciotat Station. It is said that when the film was shown for the first time, the audience was so startled by the image of the huge train coming toward them that they started to scream and run away.

Hollywood

The 1920s were the most important years for the development of modern movies. In that period, movie studios came into existence and "stars" were born. The film industry began to flourish, and Hollywood became the world's number one place for movie production, with over 800 movies being made there each year.

The 1930s are often called the Golden Era of Hollywood. It was during this era that the world saw the development of "talkies" (up to then all films had been silent), documentaries, and also Westerns.

These days, of course, modern moviegoers are used to state-of-the-art computer-generated imagery (CGI) to bring fantastical worlds and unbelievably realistic creatures to the screen in stunning 3-D. It's difficult to imagine how it can be improved upon. But as science and technology continue to advance at lightning speed, we can assume that our cinematic experience will continue to get better and better.

4 **Answer the questions.**

1 What did the first magic lanterns consist of?

2 How did Etienne Gaspar Robert scare his audiences?

3 What was the limitation of the Kinetoscope?

4 How did the Lumière brothers impress their spectators?

5 Why did Hollywood become so famous?

5 VOCABULARY **Match the highlighted words in the article with the definitions.**

1 very surprised _____
2 a round, wheel-shaped object on which film can be rolled _____
3 scary _____
4 a curved piece of glass in a camera or projector that makes objects seem closer, larger, smaller, etc. _____

5 something that acted as an early, less advanced model of another thing that will appear in the future _____
6 that you can see through _____
7 the part of a reel film projector that opens to allow light to reach the film _____
8 grow rapidly _____

WRITING

Instructions

1 Read the instructions on how to save a word file. Who do you think it has been written for and why?

2 Complete with the missing words. Then check in the instructions.

1 _____ your file is a written document, _____ you will be using a word processing program.
2 The _____ _____ you need to do is to create a new file.
3 _____ save the file, click on "file" again.
4 _____ _____ you will be able to find your file easily.
5 _____ , when you close your document, a dialogue box will appear.

3 Use a word or phrase from the list to complete each sentence.

this means | then | To | If | Finally | first thing

1 To take photos, the _____ you need is a camera.
2 _____ you're serious about photography, _____ buy the best camera.
3 Choose one with a high number of pixels – _____ that you'll have good quality images.
4 _____ find out which are the best cameras, do research on the Internet.
5 _____ , start shooting and have fun!

4 SPEAKING **Put the writing tips in order of importance. Then discuss in pairs.**

☐ Think carefully about who you are writing for.
☐ Use clear language that is easy to understand.
☐ Give the instructions in a logical order.
☐ Use a friendly, informal style.

5 Choose one of the computing processes below and write down short notes for each stage.

- how to create a folder
- how to cut and paste
- how to change the font
- how to rename a file

⊖ ◻ ⊗   ◄ ► ⌂

One of the most important things you will need to learn to do if you want to use your computer to write documents is to learn how to save a file.

1 If your file is a written document, then you will be using a word processing program such as Microsoft Word. The first thing you need to do is to create a new file. To do this, open up the program by clicking on the icon. You should be able to find this on your desktop.

2 When the program has opened, click on the icon "file" in the top left hand corner of the screen and choose "new" from the drop down menu. This will create a new document for you.

3 I would recommend saving this document, before you have written anything. This means that if your computer shuts down unexpectedly, you won't lose the file. To save the file, click on "file" again. From the drop down menu choose "save."

4 A dialogue box or window will open asking you to type in the name of your document. You will also need to choose a location for the file. Select "desktop" from the list on the left hand side of the box. This means you will be able to find your file easily when you start your computer.

5 Finally, when you close your document, a dialogue box will appear asking if you want to save any changes. Click "yes" and this will ensure you never lose any of your work.

6 Write a text (120–180 words) describing the process you chose in Exercise 5. Remember:

- decide who you are writing these instructions for (a child? a beginner? a fairly experienced user?)
- give your instructions in a logical order
- think about the tips in Exercise 4

SPEAKING

Work with a partner. Discuss the questions.

1 Why don't some people like movies with lots of special effects?
2 Make a list of movies with great special effects.
3 What's your favorite 3-D movie? Why?
4 What do you think will be the next stage in the development of movies?

6 BRINGING PEOPLE TOGETHER

READING

1 **SPEAKING** Work in pairs. Look at the photos. Describe the situations and how the people might be feeling, using these adjectives.

packed | stuffy | impatient | dull | polite | excited

> *The bus is packed, and some people don't have anywhere to sit.*

2 **SPEAKING** Choose one of the people and imagine their thoughts. Make notes. Tell your partner the person's thoughts for your partner to guess who it is.

3 **◀)) 1.32** Read and listen to the blog. Which person in the picture on page 57 do you think wrote it?

4 Read the blog again. Answer the questions.

1 How long, usually, is the writer's commute?
2 After the announcement, what was the first thing people started to talk about?
3 What did the writer find out about other people on the bus?
4 In what way(s) did people help each other?
5 Why was the nurse "welcomed as a hero"?
6 What did people do when the bus started moving?
7 What was the journey like the next day?

5 **SPEAKING** Work in pairs and discuss the questions.

1 Would this be different if it happened in your country, do you think? If so, how?
2 What other situations can you think of in which strangers might start talking to each other?
3 Can you remember a time when you started a conversation with someone you didn't know and realized that your first impressions were wrong?

Stuck in an elevator

ROLE PLAY Work in groups of four. Students A and C: Go to page 127. Students B and D: Go to page 128.

Imagine you are four strangers traveling together in an elevator. Suddenly the elevator breaks down. A repairman has been called but won't be there for half an hour. Agree together on what you should do.

The day people started TALKING

The commute to and from my art school is nothing special. I take a city bus from one side of town to the other. It's always busy, but I usually find a seat. On the bus, I read or text my friends, making sure, like everyone else, not to look at other people. Half-an-hour later, I get off.

But last Tuesday was different. It had been cloudy all day, and I'd just gotten on the bus when it started raining. Not just raining, but pouring! The bus was packed, but I squeezed into a seat and put my art bag in my lap. I was looking out the window listening to some music I'd downloaded that morning when the bus stopped in some traffic. This wasn't unusual, and I didn't think anything of it. But after about five minutes, we still hadn't moved. People were getting more and more annoyed. They were looking around and shuffling in their seats. The longer the bus stood still, the more annoyed people became. Finally, after 15 minutes, the bus driver made the dreaded announcement: "Ladies and gentlemen, there has been an accident up ahead. Unfortunately, it looks like the bus will be stuck here for a while."

Nobody wanted to get off – it was still pouring rain – so we all went back to what we were doing before. Soon there was another announcement with more information: It was a big truck that had crashed in front of us, and we were going to be there for a long time.

A loud groan filled the bus. Everyone started complaining about the crash, the rain, their bad luck, the inconvenience of the situation, traffic in our city. But then the talk started to change. People started talking about other things, real things. Complete strangers talking to each other like friends!

I was fascinated and decided to join in. I struck up a conversation with a couple of tourists sitting across from me. They were from Spain and were only in town for a few days, so I recommended some places they should see. Next, I really surprised myself by talking with a businesswoman. It turned out that there was so much more to her than a suit. She spends her weekends mountain climbing and is going to take three months off next year to climb Mount Everest. How awesome is that? I'd been wrong all my life – businesspeople are a lot cooler than I thought they were.

I decided to get up and stretch my legs. At the back of the bus, I met a woman who had been a student at my school seven years before and knew lots of my teachers. It seems they were just as strict then as they are now. She asked to see my artwork. I showed her, and she really liked it!

Throughout the bus, people offered each other food and drinks. A young woman took out her guitar, and soon people were singing along. It was so much fun. At one point, we heard there was a diabetic man in the front of the bus who needed help, and a man sitting near me jumped into action. It turns out he's a nurse and knew just what to do. When he came back to his seat, we all welcomed him as a hero.

After two and a half hours, we started moving again. Everyone clapped and cheered, and some people, strangers three hours before, even hugged.

Of course, this experience really didn't change anything. I took the bus again the next day, but none of my new "friends" were there. All the faces were different. Although people were polite, they weren't nearly as friendly as the people from the day before. So I sat down and started texting, not looking at other people, same as usual. But I'll never forget the day the bus stopped and people started talking.

■ TRAIN TO THiNK ■

Exaggeration

When we feel emotional about something, we tend to exaggerate – we call something "a brilliant idea," "the best movie ever," "an amazing journey," etc. But we often don't mean that literally. As a listener you need to be aware of exaggeration and understand what the speaker is really saying.

1   Read the example and answer the questions.

> *Last night's commute home was terrible. It was the worst trip of my life. The train was two hours late and then it stopped for ages in the middle of nowhere. I was so bored I thought I was going to go crazy. I hope today's commute won't be so bad.*

1   How many exaggerations does the speaker make?
2   What are they?
3   What does he really mean in each case?

2   SPEAKING   Work with a partner. Tell them about something really good or bad that happened to you recently. Use exaggeration.

Pronunciation

The /tʃ/ sound: negative auxiliaries + *you*
Go to page 120.

GRAMMAR
Comparatives

1 Match the sentence halves from the blog. Then read the rule and complete it with 1–5.

1 The longer the bus stood still, ☐
2 Businesspeople are a lot ☐
3 It seems my teachers were just as ☐
4 Although people were polite, they weren't nearly as ☐
5 People were getting more ☐

a friendly as the people from the day before.
b and more annoyed.
c the more annoyed people became.
d cooler than I thought they were.
e strict then as they are now.

> **RULE:**
> ● Use *a lot / far / much* + comparative to make a comparative stronger. **Sentence** ¹_____
> ● Use *just as / not nearly as / nowhere near as* + adjective + *as* to intensify a comparison. **Sentences** ²_____ and ³_____
> ● Use comparative *and* comparative + short adjectives, e.g., *hotter and hotter* to talk about how something or someone is changing and increasing in an adjective. Use *more and more* + longer adjectives, e.g., *more and more interesting*. **Sentence** ⁴_____
> ● Use *the* + comparative / *the* + comparative with short adjectives or *the more* + adjective / *the more* + adjective + clause with long adjectives to show how two events affect each other. **Sentence** ⁵_____

2 ✳ Complete the second sentence so that it has a similar meaning to the first sentence using the word given. You must use between two and five words, including the word given.

1 Today's test was much easier than yesterday's test. (nowhere)
   Today's test was _____ as yesterday's test.
2 I'm practicing the piano a lot, and I'm getting much better. (practice)
   The more I _____ I get at playing the piano.
3 The price of gasoline is going up each month. (and)
   Gas is getting _____ each month.
4 I've been seeing a lot of John recently, and I'm beginning not to like him so much. (less)
   The more I see John _____ I like him.

→ Workbook page 54

FUNCTIONS
Using intensifying comparatives

1 Look at what the writer recommended to the tourists. Match the three parts.

1 You should visit New Orleans.	a *It's easily the best* time to visit.	i And *it's even warmer* than it is now.
2 You should travel around by bus.	b *It's by far* the *most beautiful* city in the U.S.	ii And *it's a whole lot cheaper* than flying.
3 You should come back in August.	c It's the *easiest* way to travel *by far*.	iii And *it's way less* crowded than Boston.

2 Make recommendations to visitors to your country using the sentences in Exercise 1 to help you. Then compare with a partner.

You should go by car. It's easily the best way to see the country and it's a lot less expensive than flying.

VOCABULARY
Ways of speaking

1 Which one of these sentences was probably *not* said on the bus in the blog on page 57?

1 "Do you know what's wrong with the bus?"
2 "You should definitely visit Miami."
3 "There's never anywhere to sit on these buses."
4 "Hi, my name is Raffa, and this is Clara."
5 "We're sorry to say the bus has a problem."
6 "It was me. I had the last piece of chocolate cake."

2 Match the sentences in Exercise 1 with the speaker's communicative aim in each one.

☐ to recommend   ☐ to confess
☐ to introduce   ☐ to inquire
☐ to announce   ☐ to complain

3 Use the suffixes to complete the table.

~~-ation~~ | -ion | -tion | -y | -ment | -t

0	to recommend	to make a *recommendation*
1	to confess	to make a _____
2	to introduce	to make an _____
3	to inquire	to make an _____
4	to announce	to make an _____
5	to complain	to make a _____

4 Choose three of the functions above and write an example of it. Read them to your partner to guess.

This is Harry.   *You're making an introduction.*

→ Workbook page 56

LISTENING

1 Put the pictures in order to make a story about Sophie and Rob. Compare with a partner.

2 🔊 1.35 Listen to the story Rob's brother tells the guests. Check ✳ your ideas in Exercise 1.

3 🔊 1.35 Listen again and complete the sentences.

1 Sophie is pretty shy, but she has lots of _____.
2 The first time Sophie saw "Train Man" they were on the _____ waiting for the train.
3 Sophie told all her _____ about "Train Man."
4 Sophie finally made contact with "Train Man" by giving him a _____.
5 She learned his name was Rob when he sent her an _____.
6 Sophie was disappointed to find out that Rob had a _____.
7 Rob sent Sophie a second email about a _____ after he sent the first one.
8 Rob proposed, and he and Sophie got _____ during a train trip across Australia.

VOCABULARY
Love and relationships

1 Complete the phrases from the story with the missing verbs.

get | break | ask | get
fall | go | go | be

1 to _____ in love (with someone) – to develop very strong feelings for someone
2 to _____ up (with someone) – to end a relationship
3 to _____ married (to someone) – to become husband and wife
4 to _____ engaged (to someone) – to agree to get married
5 to _____ (someone) out – to invite someone to do something (with romance in mind!)
6 to _____ out (together / with someone) – to become boyfriend and girlfriend
7 to _____ on a date (with someone) – to do something together (to see if you like each other)
8 to _____ over (someone) – to not be sad anymore about an ex

2 Use phrases in Exercise 1 in the correct tense to complete the story of Sophie and Rob.

Rob finally [1]_____ with his girlfriend. When he felt that he [2]_____ her, he asked Sophie out in an email. She was really happy, and they [3]_____ a few days later. They got along really well and started [4]_____ with each other. They quickly [5]_____ with each other. On vacation in Australia, Rob asked Sophie to marry him. She said yes! Now, they [6]_____, and Rob's brother is giving the toast at their reception.

3 SPEAKING Work in pairs. Think of a famous couple. Tell their story to another pair using the phrases above.

Workbook page 56 ▶

READING

1 **Look at the photo and answer the questions.**

1 What are the people doing?
2 Why do you think they are doing it?

2 **Read the article and check your ideas. Explain the play on words in the last sentence.**

3 **Read the article again and mark the sentences T (true), F (false), or DS (doesn't say).**

1 Pete Frates wanted to play professional baseball. ☐
2 He was diagnosed with an illness called ALS in 2014. ☐
3 If you did the Ice Bucket Challenge, you didn't have to pay any money. ☐
4 You had to film yourself doing the challenge. ☐
5 Barack Obama refused to give any money to the charity. ☐
6 Some people felt the Ice Bucket Challenge was a bit dangerous. ☐
7 Nearly 15% of the U.K. population donated money through the Ice Bucket Challenge. ☐
8 ALS research benefited from the craze, but other charities were negatively affected. ☐

SPEAKING

Work in pairs and discuss the questions.

1 Do you remember the Ice Bucket Challenge? Did you, or anyone you know, take part in it?
2 Do you think it was a good idea? Why or why not?
3 What would you have said to someone who refused to take part?
4 What other examples can you think of where people have used social media to raise money for charity?

An Ice Cold Summer

In the summer of 2014, a weird and wonderful craze swept across the world. Everywhere you looked people were pouring buckets of freezing water over their heads. The craze soon had a name – the Ice Bucket Challenge – and the idea behind it was to raise money for charity.

Despite the popularity of the challenge, not many people knew where it came from. In fact, it was the idea of an American named Pete Frates. He had been a promising college baseball player who seemed to have a bright future with the Boston Red Sox. His career was cut short, however, when he fell ill with a disease called amyotrophic lateral sclerosis (ALS, for short). ALS attacks the nervous system and can cause speech problems and paralysis. It can also kill. Frates wanted to do something to raise both money and awareness to help sufferers of ALS. He had a simple but brilliant idea.

The idea was to choose a couple of friends and challenge them to pour a bucket of freezing water over their heads. If they did it, then they paid $10 to the charity. If they refused, they paid $100. To prove they had done it, they had 24 hours to post a video of their challenge online. Then it was their turn to nominate two more people and challenge them.

Soon, the Ice Bucket Challenge had gone viral, with plenty of celebrities worldwide joining in, including Usain Bolt, Lady Gaga, Oprah Winfrey, Taylor Swift, Cristiano Ronaldo, and even former U.S. President George W. Bush. U.S. President Barack Obama and U.K. Prime Minister David Cameron were also challenged, although they both refused to do it and donated the $100 instead. All in all, more than 2,500,000 videos were posted on social media sites from at least 150 different countries. And millions of dollars were donated to the ALS Foundation.

Not everyone viewed the Ice Bucket Challenge in a positive light, however. Some people felt that it put too much pressure on people who did not want to (or maybe could not afford to) donate money. If you were chosen by a friend and decided you did not want to take part, you were seen as being mean and not joining the fun. Some misunderstood the challenge, thinking that they didn't have to donate if they poured the ice water on themselves. Some people did the challenge but didn't donate. One study found that even though over 15 percent of the British population had done the challenge, only 10 percent actually gave any money to charity. Other people pointed out that so much attention on one charity pulls attention away from other, equally worthwhile charities. ALS research profited, but other research efforts received less money than usual because of it.

So, was the Ice Bucket challenge a good thing or not? That will always depend on who you talk to. Nevertheless, for a few hot months back in the summer of 2014, the Ice Bucket Challenge brought millions of people from all over the planet together for a "cool" cause.

GRAMMAR
Linkers of contrast

1 **Read the example sentences about the article and use them to complete the rule.**

1 Most people thought the Ice Bucket Challenge was brilliant. **However**, there were people who disagreed.

2 **Despite** its popularity, many people didn't know where the idea had come from.

3 Pete Frates found the time to raise money for charity **in spite of** being very ill.

4 **Although** he was challenged, President Obama decided not to pour water over his head.

5 I didn't do the challenge **even though** four of my friends nominated me.

6 Many people did the challenge without donating. **Nevertheless**, the charity made a lot of money.

> **RULE:** To contrast ideas and facts, we use these linking words: *although, even though, however, despite, in spite of,* and *nevertheless.*
>
> 1 *Despite* and _____ are followed by a noun phrase or a gerund. They can be used at the beginning or in the middle of a sentence.
>
> 2 *Although* and _____ are followed by a full clause. They can be used at the beginning or in the middle of a sentence.
>
> 3 *However* and _____ introduce the contrasting idea and come at the beginning of a new sentence. They are followed by a comma.

2 **Rewrite the sentences using the word in parentheses.**

0 I didn't know anyone at the party, but I still had a good time. (in spite of)
In spite of not knowing anyone at the party, I still had a good time.

1 I studied hard for the test. I failed it. (despite)

2 He doesn't earn a lot of money. He gives a lot to charity. (However)

3 I'd seen the movie before. I still really enjoyed it. (although)

4 I started to eat less. I didn't lose any weight. (in spite of)

5 It wasn't very warm. We had a good time at the beach. (Nevertheless)

6 I don't speak a word of Chinese. I understood what he said. (even though)

3 **Rewrite this idea using each of the linkers from the rule box.**

I felt really tired. I stayed up until midnight to celebrate the new year.

Workbook page 55

■ THiNK VALUES ■
Doing good

1 **Work in groups of four. You are going to run a fundraising challenge for a charity. Use these points to help organize your ideas.**

1 Decide on a charity.
- Why are you choosing this charity?
- What will the charity use this money for?

2 Decide on a challenge
- What is the challenge?
- How are people chosen for the challenge?
- What do you have to do if you refuse to do it?

3 Think of a famous person to get involved.
- Why this person?
- What do you want them to do?

4 Extras
- What other things can you do to help your campaign? (T-shirts, write a song, etc.)

2 SPEAKING **Present your ideas to the class. Each student in your group should talk about one of the points in Exercise 1.**

Literature

1 Look at the photos and read the introduction to the extract. What do you think Vic is thinking about when he's waiting for the bus with Ingrid?

2 🔊 1.36 Read and listen to the extract and check your ideas.

A kind of loving by Stan Barstow

Vic Brown is a young drafter at an engineering company in northern England in the 1950s. He lives with his mother and father. He is attracted to one of the administrative assistants at the company – Ingrid Rothwell – and one day, as they leave work, they run into each other and start walking to the bus stop together.

'm going your way," she says.

I hold the door open for her and get a gorgeous whiff of her scent as she goes by. We say good night to the commissionaire and walk off down the lane. […]

It seems there's a lot I don't know and she starts to bring me up to date. I don't have to make the conversation tonight; she just rolls it out. She's as full of scandal as the Sunday papers and by the time we get to the bus stop I know more about the people who work at Whittaker's than I've learned all the time I've been there.

I get both fares into town and she says, "That makes us quits," and smiles.

She picks up where she left off and starts chattering again; but I'm not really listening now. My mind's working like mad on how I can make the most of this chance. I try to think of a way to get started and all the time the bus is tearing down the road into town. When I see the Grammar School sail by I kind of panic because I know we'll be in the station any minute now.

"Look, there's something I –" And she starts talking again at the same time. We both stop. "Go on," I say.

"I was just going to ask you if you'd seen that new musical *Rise and Shine* at the Palace," she says. "I was wondering what it was like."

I haven't a clue what it's like, to be honest, but I say, "I think it's good," and I'm thinking, Now, now, now: what are you waiting for? "I was thinking of going to see it myself one night this week, as a matter of fact," I say. This is another fib, but I don't care. I have to clear my throat. "P'raps … er, mebbe you'd like to come with me … see it together …"

She says, "Oh!" just as if it was the last thing she'd have thought of and I begin to think how I can pass it off if she turns me down. "Well, when?"

I can hardly sit still in the seat. I want to jump up and shout, I'm that excited. "I'd thought of going tomorrow, but any night 'ud suit me really."

"Tomorrow's New Year's Eve," she says, "and I'm going to a party. Can you make it Wednesday?"

"All right." Wednesday, Thursday, Friday, Saturday or Sunday. I can make it any night or all of them. I just want it to be soon.

"Wednesday, then," she says, and I nod. "Wednesday."

Before the bus pulls into the station we've fixed up what time we'll meet and where and everything. And to think, only this morning I wouldn't have given a bent penny for my chances. But that's how things work out sometimes. Wednesday … I just don't know how I'll live till then.

But course I do, and now here I am waiting on the corner at twenty-five to eight. She's late, but only five minutes, and I was here ten minutes early to make sure I didn't miss her so that makes it seem more.

3 Read the extract again. Answer the questions.

1 What does Ingrid talk about as she and Vic walk to the bus stop?

2 What is Vic thinking about as the bus approaches the station?

3 What two things does Vic say to Ingrid that aren't really true?

4 Why does Vic want "to jump up and shout?"

5 Why does it seem to Vic that Ingrid is later than she is?

4 VOCABULARY **Match the highlighted words and phrases in the extract with the definitions.**

1 a lie; something someone says that's not true

2 agreeing that no one owes anything to another person

3 things about other people that are shocking

4 be available (to meet or to do something)

5 someone who does drawings of machines, new buildings, etc.

6 a slight smell

7 going very, very fast

8 talking a long time about not very important things

5 SPEAKING **Work in pairs. Discuss the questions.**

1 Vic doesn't find it easy to ask Ingrid out. Can you think of other times when people find it difficult to say what they want to say?

2 Do you think Ingrid will turn up to meet Vic? Why or why not?

WRITING
An essay

1 Read the essay, which is out of order, quickly. Does the author agree or disagree with the essay title? Why?

2 Read the paragraph functions and write A–D in the boxes below.

1 introduction

2 argument supporting the idea

3 argument against the idea

4 the writer's final opinion

3 Complete with the missing linkers. Then check in the essay.

1 Because it's so much easier, _____, more and more people are using social media for that purpose.

2 _____, people are getting tired of constantly being asked to donate.

3 _____, these requests often come from strangers or friends of friends. They lack the personal touch.

4 _____, people are starting to ignore these appeals.

5 _____, I still believe that social media can be a really useful way of raising money for charity.

6 _____, it's no surprise that more and more people are using social media to raise money for charity.

4 Look at the essay title and make notes.

Social media brings people together.

Introduction: _____
For: _____
Against: _____
My conclusion: _____

5 Write your essay in 140–190 words.

Social media is the best way of raising money for charity

A Nevertheless, I still believe that social media can be a really useful way of raising money for charity. We just need to be careful how we use it and make sure we don't use it too often.

B When my mother was a child, she used to take part in different campaigns to raise money for good causes. She would knock on people's doors asking them to pledge money. Then, at the end of the campaign, she had to return to collect the money. These days people use social media to ask for financial pledges. With one click people can donate immediately. Collecting money for charity has never been easier.

C Because it's so much easier, however, more and more people are using social media for that purpose. As a consequence, people are getting tired of constantly being asked to donate every time they check their email or want to post an update. Furthermore, these requests often come from strangers or friends of friends. They lack the personal touch. As a result, people are starting to ignore these appeals.

D Social media is a huge part of people's lives. It's often the quickest and easiest way of keeping in touch with friends or sharing thoughts with a wider audience. Therefore, it's no surprise that more and more people are using social media to raise money for charity. But is that always a good idea?

READING AND USE OF ENGLISH
Part 7: Matching

Workbook page 61 ➤

1 You are going to read an article in which four teenagers talk about how they met their best friend. For questions 1–10, choose from the teenagers (A–D). The teenagers may be chosen more than once.

Which teenager

1   feels that they met their best friend at the perfect time?

2   has changed their attitude about best friends several times?

3   has known their best friend for most of their life?

4   felt an instant connection with their best friend?

5   thinks it can be a good thing to have a small number of very close friends?

6   gets along with their best friend because they can discuss different topics?

7   feels that their best friend also helped them to get along better with people at school?

8   thinks that distance helps keep a relationship healthy?

9   made best friends with the new kid in class right away?

10   thinks it's a good thing that their best friend doesn't know their other friends?

A Dom

My best friend is Luis, and I've only known him for about three months. I met Luis at a youth club, and I knew immediately that he was going to be a great friend. We share exactly the same sense of humor. We like the same bands. I'm really interested in politics, and he shares exactly the same concerns as I do. It was great to finally be able to talk about something other than football and girls. Don't get me wrong, I still like talking about those things, but it's good to have a change. Also, because Luis doesn't go to the same school as me, it means that we don't waste time talking about other friends.

B Janice

I've had a lot of best friends. I remember when I was a kid I'd have a new best friend every week. Then when I was a little older, I thought it was silly to have one best friend and just tried to have as many friends as I could. Recently though, I realized that, although it's good to have lots of friends, it's good to have one or two extra special ones that you know will always be there for you no matter what. I guess, at the moment, Maribel would be that friend. I really haven't known her very long, probably about a year at the most. She was the new kid in school, and at first I wasn't very friendly to her at all, probably because I already had my gang of friends. But she was in lots of my classes, and I started to get to know her better and realized she was really cool.

C Anna

I still remember the first time I met Robert. I must have been about 10 or 11. I was at school when the teacher introduced him as the new student and told him to sit next to me. We started talking immediately and have hardly stopped talking since. Mom says I didn't have a lot of friends at that age and found it difficult to get along with the other kids. She says that Robert helped me find the confidence I needed to make new friends. Now we're in high school, and we still spend lots of time together. Of course, I tend to hang out with the girls and Robert hangs out with the boys, but we often meet up after school or on weekends.

D Charlie

I've known my best friend Tom since I was two. Of course, I don't remember him from then, but we met because our dads took us to the same park to play when we were toddlers. They became best friends, and we grew up almost as brothers. When I was about seven, Mom and Dad moved away, but they kept in touch with Tom's parents, so Tom and I would still see each other over the summer. These days we keep in touch on Facebook, and we text each other a lot. It's great having someone who knows you so well, and I think the fact that we live more than 100 kilometers apart means that we've become even better friends. We don't get tired of each other because we don't see each other all the time.

TEST YOURSELF

VOCABULARY

1 **Complete the sentences with the words in the list. There are four extra words.**

stream | backup | zip | upgrade | craze | broke | introduced | going
recommendation | confessed | access | startled | complained | lens

1 Jake is feeling really down. He just _____ up with his girlfriend.
2 My friends Alex and Nancy have been _____ out together for over a year.
3 I asked him four times to give me my watch back, and then he _____ that he'd lost it.
4 I know who Paul is, but I've never been _____ to him.
5 The file was so big that I had to _____ it to send it by email.
6 My computer runs my new graphics program very slowly. I need to _____ it.
7 I almost lost everything when my computer crashed, but luckily I had a _____ of most of it.
8 The old lady was so _____ when the dog barked at her that she dropped her groceries.
9 The neighbors _____ about the noise at our party.
10 Steve said this tablet was great, so I bought it on his _____.

/10

GRAMMAR

2 **Complete the sentences with the phrases in the list. There is one extra phrase.**

succeeded in | been able | managed to | nowhere near as
wasn't allowed to | even though | didn't have to

1 I've never visited the museum _____ I live very close to it.
2 My uncle took lots of lessons, but he never _____ learning to drive.
3 My mom _____ go out with friends until she was sixteen.
4 The sequel is _____ good as the first movie.
5 Dave had already asked Mom about the trip, so I _____ ask her.
6 My aunt hurt her hand last month. She hasn't _____ to play the piano since then.

3 **Find and correct the mistake in each sentence.**

1 We ran as fast as we could, but we didn't manage get there in time.
2 Despite earns a good salary, Mario says he never has enough money.
3 Nicole's parents weren't as strict with her brother than they were with her.
4 Nevertheless, Barry's French isn't great, he understood a lot of the movie.
5 It is very kind of you, but you don't need pick me up. I can walk to the restaurant.
6 James always does well on tests, although never studying.

/12

FUNCTIONAL LANGUAGE

4 **Choose the correct options.**

1 A I think Demi Lovato's latest album is by *far* / *way* the best album she's ever released.
  B I agree. It's *lot* / *even* better than her last one.
2 A I *must* / *need* go home now. I still have homework to finish for tomorrow.
  B No, you *mustn't* / *don't need to* do it for tomorrow – it's a holiday. Remember?
3 A Do your parents *let* / *allow* you stay out as late as you want?
  B Yes, but only on weekends, and I *have* / *must* to tell them what time I'll be home.
4 A I love this game. It's *easily* / *even* the best game I've ever played.
  B No way! Prince of Shadows is a *whole* / *good* lot better than this.

/8

MY SCORE **/30**

| 22 – 30 |
| 10 – 21 |
| 0 – 9 |

7 | ALWAYS LOOK ON THE BRIGHT SIDE

OBJECTIVES

FUNCTIONS: cheering someone up

GRAMMAR: ways of referring to the future (review); future continuous; future perfect

VOCABULARY: phrases to talk about the future: *about to, off to, (period of time) away from*; feelings about future events

READING

1 Look at the photos. What do you think the message of each one is?

2 SPEAKING Read statements A and B. Discuss the differences in their reactions in class. Then say who is more like you: the person who wrote statement A or the one who wrote B.

A My best friend has moved to another country. I'll never get over it. I won't find anybody that I like as much as her, so I won't even try to find a new friend. What if I found one, and she moved away, too?

B My best friend just moved to another country. That's great for her. I'm definitely going to stay in touch, and I'm looking forward to hearing stories about her new life. And who knows? One day I might even be able to visit her.

3 Read through the blog quickly and answer the questions.

1 What does the blogger call her character?

2 What does he do for a living?

3 Is he an optimist or a pessimist?

4 ◀)) 2.02 Read the blog again and listen. Mark the statements T (true) or F (false). Then work with a partner and correct the false statements.

1 The blogger is concerned with her own attitudes and those of her friends. ☐

2 The main reason the blogger writes this post is to share an exciting story. ☐

3 The main character of the story is a man whose attitude about life changed after he was attacked. ☐

4 The robber went to the store intending to kill the man who worked there. ☐

5 On the way to the hospital, the man was feeling calm because of the support he got from the paramedics. ☐

6 When Jim arrived in the operating room, the staff didn't seem hopeful. ☐

7 Jim made a joke, but no one found it funny. ☐

8 The blogger thinks that the positive attitude Jim showed in a difficult situation helped save his life. ☐

5 SPEAKING Work in pairs. Discuss the questions.

1 Did you like the story the blogger told? Do you agree that Jim's positive attitude helped save his life?

2 Do you think a story like this could change people's attitudes? Why or why not?

Me, Myself, & My Take on the World

Take #17: It's all about the positivity

Today's take is about attitude. So many of my friends are total pessimists. You know, the kind of people who think, "There's a dark cloud up there. It's going to rain soon." Guys, we all need to work on our attitudes. It matters how we see things!

I read a story recently that I want to share with you, and if you're a pessimist (like my friends) maybe it'll change your attitude a little, too. It's about this guy, I've forgotten his name, let's call him Jim. He was kind of a born optimist, always in a good mood.

Jim owned a store, and a customer once asked him how he managed to stay so friendly and positive all the time. His answer was, "When I wake up in the morning, I know that the day will have good and bad moments for me, but whatever happens, I'm going to choose to be in a good mood."

Then one day, something terrible happened. Jim was about to leave the store when an armed robber came in, held him up at gunpoint, and made him open the safe. As he was trying to open it, Jim's hand slipped. The robber saw this and probably thought, "He's about to attack me!" The robber panicked and fired his gun.

Jim was rushed to the hospital. In the ambulance, he felt fine because the paramedic kept telling him, "Don't worry. I'm sure you'll be OK. As soon as we get to the hospital, the doctors will take care of you."

But when Jim was in the operating room and he saw the faces of the doctors and nurses, he got the feeling that they thought he was already dead. He knew he needed to do something to change their attitude.

There was a nurse who was asking him lots of questions, very fast. One question was, "Are you allergic to anything?" "Yes!" Jim said loudly and everybody stopped what they were doing. There was total silence. "Bullets!" Jim said, and all the doctors and nurses burst out laughing. And then Jim added, "Please operate on me thinking that I'll live, and not that I'll die."

Jim survived, thanks to the skill of the doctors and nurses. But what also helped was that he managed to remain an optimist even in the most desperate moment of his life.

So listen up, readers. Let's try and be positive more often. Actually, I'm about to do that right now. I have a piano lesson at four today. Not my idea really – it's my parents who think it's good for me to learn a musical instrument. But I'll be a good daughter. Maybe my mom and dad are right. I'll keep an open mind. I'll choose to find something positive about playing the piano. I will! Anyway, I'd better go. My bus leaves in five minutes. Oh, and while I'm thinking about it, I'm off to the beach on Tuesday – family vacation – so I'll post my next update two weeks from now.

■ TRAIN TO THINK

Learning to see things from a different perspective

How we see a situation influences how we feel about it and how we behave in it. Learning to look at things from a more optimistic perspective can have a positive influence on the outcome of a situation.

1   Read what these people have experienced when trying to look at things from a different perspective. Say what and who helped them change their attitude.

For a long time, I used to worry about everything all the time. I even used to worry about not finding anything to worry about. Then we had this discussion in class, and one of my teachers told us a saying I'll never forget. It may sound ridiculous, but it really helped me change my attitude. It basically says, "For every problem under the sun, there either is a solution or there isn't. If there is, think about it until you find it. If there isn't, then let it go."

I never really believed in myself. I always thought everybody else was better than me. One day I went out with a group of friends, and we met this guy who seemed really nice. But then I noticed that he started to make fun of the things I said. I became quiet and started to feel bad about myself. When I spoke to my best friend afterward, she just said, "So what? That guy's strange, but that's him, not you." So I decided to ignore the guy, and soon he stopped making fun of me. More importantly, I felt better about myself.

2   SPEAKING Write down two difficult situations where you could usefully apply either of the two perspectives above. Compare with a partner.

GRAMMAR

Ways of referring to the future (review)

1 **Look at the sentences from the blog. Then complete the rule with** *be going to* **(A),** *will* **(B),** *the present continuous* **(C), or** *the simple present* **(D).**

1 There's a dark cloud up there. It**'s going to** rain soon!
2 I **have** a piano lesson at four today.
3 **As soon as** we **get** to the hospital, the doctors **will** take care of you.
4 **I'll** post my next update two weeks from now.
5 My bus **leaves** in five minutes.
6 Don't worry. I'm sure **you'll** be OK.
7 Whatever happens, I**'m going to** choose to be in a good mood.
8 When I wake up in the morning, I know that the day **will have** good and bad moments for me.

> **RULE:** We use:
> 1 _____ to talk about future facts
> 2 _____ to talk about events that are part of a timetable or schedule
> 3 _____ to make evidence-based predictions
> 4 _____ to make predictions based on thoughts and opinions
> 5 _____ to talk about plans and intentions
> 6 _____ to refer to definite arrangements
> 7 _____ immediately after time expressions like *when*, *before*, *after*, *until*, and *as soon as* when referring to future events
> 8 _____ to refer to spontaneous decisions and offers

2 **Complete the sentences using the most appropriate form of the verbs in parentheses. Sometimes more than one form is possible.**

1 My dad _____ on the eight o'clock flight from Mexico City tomorrow. (arrive)
2 Careful! You've filled that glass too full. You _____ (spill) it.
3 I think it _____ probably _____ a lot this weekend. It's that time of year. (rain)
4 We _____ friends on Saturday. (see)
5 I'm sorry, but can I call you back later? The movie _____ in two minutes. (start)
6 We'll stop at the market before we _____ home. (go)
7 When I get paid, I _____ myself a new camera. (buy)
8 Today's lunch break _____ five minutes shorter than usual. (be)

Workbook page 64

VOCABULARY

Phrases to talk about the future: *about to, off to, (period of time) away from*

1 **All of these sentences refer to the future. Which sentence talks about:**

a future travel plans?
b something happening relatively soon?
c the very immediate future?

1 He**'s about to** call me.
2 I**'m off** to Spain on Tuesday.
3 She's just **one semester away from** graduating.

> **LOOK!**
> • *be about to* + verb
> • *be off to* + place
> • *be* + (time period) + *away from* + noun / verb + *-ing*

2 **Choose the correct options.**

1 Although this is a serious situation, Jennifer looks as if she's *about to / off to* start laughing.
2 I'm *off to / about to* the supermarket in five minutes. Do you want anything?
3 Careful! You're *one second away from / about to* knock the glass over.
4 My friends are *off to / about to* get a big surprise!
5 They're *off to / a day away from* France on their vacation.
6 We're *seconds away from / about to* winning the Super Bowl!

Workbook page 66

LISTENING

1 🔊 2.03 **Listen to the conversation and answer the questions.**

1 Complete the phrase: "Every _____ has a silver lining."
2 Explain this phrase in your own words.

2 🔊 2.03 **Listen again and note Alex's and Colin's responses.**

Alex is cut from the football team:

_____
_____

It's raining, and the beach is closed:

_____
_____

Football practice is going to be difficult:

_____
_____

3 SPEAKING Work in pairs. Think of other "silver linings" for the scenarios in the listening. How many can you come up with?

GRAMMAR
Future continuous

1 **Look at the examples from the recording. Then choose the correct option in the rule and complete with *be*, *-ing*.**

1 On Tuesday afternoon you and the other guys **will be rolling around** in the mud.

2 I'll **be sitting** in the new coffee shop downtown.

> **RULE:** To talk about an action that will be in progress [1]*after / around* a specific future time, we use the future continuous. *will* + [2]_____ + the [3]_____ form of the verb.

2 **Complete the conversation with the correct form of the verb – future or future continuous.**

JESSIE   This time tomorrow, my dad and I [1]_____ (sit) on a train.

PAULA   Really? Where are you going? Anywhere nice?

JESSIE   Yes. Dad's invited me to go to LA with him on Saturday.

PAULA   Wow!

JESSIE   Tomorrow morning we [2]_____ (walk) around the city shopping.

PAULA   Great! I [3]_____ (call) you on Saturday afternoon to hear all about it.

JESSIE   Well, on Saturday afternoon we [4]_____ (watch) the Los Angeles Angels beating the New York Mets. I can't wait! You know how much I like baseball.

PAULA   And you [5]_____ (come) home happy and relaxed. Lucky you.

JESSIE   Well, I hope so. It's an important game for the Angels.

PAULA   It all sounds wonderful. So what time's your train tomorrow?

JESSIE   Six o'clock.

PAULA   All right, at 6:30, I [6]_____ (think) of you.

JESSIE   And I [7]_____ (post) some photos on Facebook – if I remember.

Future perfect

3 **Look at the example sentences and complete the rule with *have*, *past participle*, and *will*.**

1 By then I **will have become** a big basketball star.

2 The rain **will have made** everything fresh and clean.

> **RULE:** To talk about an action that will finish some time between now and a specified time in the future, we use the future perfect. We often use it with the preposition *by*:
> [1]_____ + [2]_____ + [3]_____

4 **Choose the correct tense to complete the sentences.**

1 By the time my mom comes back from work, I'll *be finishing / have finished* my homework.

2 By 2030, psychologists will *be finding / have found* ways to help pessimists feel more optimistic.

3 Don't call after 10 p.m. I'll *be sleeping / have slept*.

4 This time tomorrow morning we'll *be flying / have flown* to Singapore. We land in the afternoon.

5 When I graduate, I will *be spending / have spent* six years at this school.

6 You can find Ms. Green in Room 305. She'll *be teaching / have taught* there until noon.

7 We're going to watch movies all day Saturday. By the end of the day, we will *be watching / have watched* more than five movies!

8 The band will *be touring / have toured* for six months later this year to promote their new album.

> Workbook page 65

SPEAKING

1 **Work in groups of four. Read the situations and think of "silver linings." Make notes.**

- Student A: Your best friend completely forgets your birthday.
- Student B: Someone spills orange juice on your new shirt.
- Student C: You fail your history test.
- Student D: Your country doesn't qualify for the World Cup.

2 **Take turns talking about the "silver linings" in your situations. Give a point for each correct use of the future continuous or the future perfect. Award five points for the most imaginative answer.**

READING

1 Read this page from a website. Who is it for? What are the two worries mentioned by people who've posted on the website?

2 Read it again. Match the responses with the worries. There is one extra response.

3 Read it once more and answer the questions in your notebook.

    1 What does the writer have in common with the two worriers?

    2 What is the difference between the writer and the two worriers?

    3 Are the two worriers equally pessimistic? Why or why not?

    4 What is the writer referring to in the third answer by saying, "And remember the rainbow!"

4 SPEAKING Discuss in class.

    1 What kind of person is the owner of this website? Would you like to know them? Why or why not?

    2 How would you react if you were in the situation of one of the two worriers?

    3 Do you think quotations can cheer you up when you're down?

    4 Which of the three quotes do you like most? Why?

    5 Look at the extra quote. What kind of problem could this quote be an answer to?

QUOTATIONSforWORRIERS

"You'll never find a rainbow if you look down!" Who said that? No, it wasn't me. It was Charlie Chaplin, and I love it. You must know that I wasn't exactly born an optimist myself. I was actually quite a worrier until I discovered the power of inspirational quotes. Try me. Send me a worry, and I'll send you a quote – free. If you like the quote, please let me know. Positive messages help me, too.

A shouldIstayorshouldIgo?

Hi. I don't know what to do. My uncle lives in the U.S., and he and his wife have invited me to stay with them next summer. Sounds cool, doesn't it? But I'm worried there won't be anyone my age to hang out with. They live in a small town, and they don't have any kids of their own. It may sound weird, but I feel like whatever I decide, I'll probably regret it later!

B Drummer boy

Help needed! I got a drum kit for my 16th birthday. There's a band at my school. They're great, but their drummer, Keith, is leaving at the end of the school year – his family is moving to another town. The band has asked me if I want to audition, and Keith has offered to teach me. But I'm not sure I'll be good enough. I don't think I should get my hopes up. I'd be so disappointed if I didn't get in.

1 ☐ Hmm, yes, I understand that it's not an easy situation. But I don't think that means you should just sit around complaining. Maybe what Anne Frank said will help you to be more optimistic: "How wonderful it is that nobody needs to wait a single moment before starting to improve the world."

2 ☐ This one is for you, and it's from Mahatma Gandhi. I'll say no more. It's all in the quote. "Man often becomes what he believes himself to be. If I keep on saying to myself that I cannot do a certain thing, it is possible that I may end by really becoming incapable of doing it. On the contrary, if I have the belief that I can do it, I shall surely acquire the capacity to do it even if I may not have it at the beginning."

3 ☐ My quote for you is from Winston Churchill: "A pessimist sees the difficulty in every opportunity; an optimist sees the opportunity in every difficulty." Even if you are right, there are probably about a million things you can do there that you can't do at home. So I'd say, go! And remember the rainbow!

VOCABULARY

Feelings about future events

1 Work in pairs. Make a list of five situations or events that can make you feel worried.

2 Read these other extracts from QUOTATIONSforWORRIERS. What event do you think each extract refers to?

> **A** It's a big game, and **I'm feeling really nervous.** If we win, we'll be in first place. I'm excited, but **I'm also a little concerned** about our chances. I mean, they're a good team.

> **B** **I'm really looking forward to** it. To be honest, I'll probably be old enough to be the other students' mother and that will feel pretty weird, but overall I don't care. **I've got a really good feeling about** this. Any suggestions for how I can bridge the age gap with my new classmates?

> **C** I'm absolutely **dreading** it, and I'm sure I'm going to fail. I haven't done any work on it, and **I just don't know where to start. It's a nightmare – I'm really worried** about it.

> **D** I don't know why **I'm getting so worked up.** I've gone to him lots of times before, and he's really good, but **I've just got a bad feeling about** it this time. I think I need to have one of my teeth pulled.

3 Look at the words in bold in Exercise 2 and use them to complete each list. If needed, use a dictionary to help you.

expressing optimism	expressing pessimism / worry
I'm really looking forward to	*I'm dreading*

4 Match the expressions in Exercise 3 with the events you listed in Exercise 1 in which you might feel them.

> Workbook page 66 ➤

FUNCTIONS

Cheering someone up

1 🔊 2.04 Complete the sentences with the words in the list. Then listen and check.

down | cheer | light | hang | bright

1 _____ up! Things will be better in the morning.

2 _____ in there. Final exams will be over soon.

3 Don't let it get you _____. It's not the end of the world.

4 I can see that losing the game is really bothering you, but try to look on the _____ side – it's early in the season.

5 This semester has been really difficult, but I'm finally starting to see some _____ at the end of the tunnel!

2 Work in pairs. What would you say to each person A–D in Vocabulary Exercise 2? Use the phrases in Exercise 1, above.

■ THiNK SELF-ESTEEM ■

What cheers me up

1 Which of these things help you feel better when you are down? Think of two more of your own.

- ☐ talking things through with a family member
- ☐ doing something outdoors
- ☐ hanging out with your best friend
- ☐ watching a good movie
- ☐ going to a party
- ☐ eating chocolate
- ☐ shopping
- ☐ sleeping

2 How do each of these things help cheer you up? Make notes.

doing something outdoors — forget about problems.

3 SPEAKING Work in pairs. Discuss your answers.

> When I've had an argument with my mom, I always like going for a long walk by myself. It helps me see things more clearly.

WRITING

A short story

1 You are going to write a story that ends with the words, "Every cloud has a silver lining."

Think of:
- an unfortunate incident
- an unexpected positive outcome
- how it changed the main character's life

2 Write your story in 140–190 words.

The contest

1 Look at the photos and answer the questions.

1 What do you think Liam wants to do?
2 What does Emma think of his idea?

2 🔊2.05 Now read and listen to the photostory. Check your ideas.

LIAM Oh, and look at this one, Emma. This was the sunset outside our house yesterday. What do you think? Pretty amazing, isn't it?

EMMA Um. Yes, it's pretty … um. It's pretty! It's the best one you've shown me so far.

LIAM I'm really getting into photography. And I've only been doing it for two months or so. It's amazing what great photos you can get just with your phone.

EMMA Yes. Yes, I guess so.

LIAM Anyway, there's a photo contest next month at school that I'm thinking of entering. First prize is a tablet. I think I've got a real shot at it.

EMMA That's great. Go for it!

1

EMMA Then he tells me he's thinking of entering the school photo contest. I don't want to be negative, but there's no way he's good enough.

JUSTIN Yeah, he showed me some of his photos the other day, too – pictures of some trees that he thought looked cool, but I wasn't that impressed. They were out of focus, for starters!

NICOLE He hasn't shown me any of his photos yet. Are they really that bad?

JUSTIN I'm afraid so. They're the kind of thing you might post online and get a few likes, but they're certainly not going to win any contests.

EMMA But that's just it. He thinks he's got a shot. I don't want him to get his hopes up.

JUSTIN He has no shot at all.

NICOLE So, what are we going to do? We can't let him make a fool of himself.

EMMA I don't know. I tried to tell him they weren't that good, gently of course, but you know Liam.

JUSTIN Yeah, it can be difficult to tell him things sometimes. He's always so enthusiastic.

NICOLE Well, we have to do something.

2

EMMA I've got an idea.

NICOLE What?

EMMA Well, you said he hadn't shown you any of his pictures yet. Why don't you ask to see them and then tell him the truth?

NICOLE Oh, thanks. So I get to be the bad guy. And what if I don't think they're bad?

EMMA Fair enough. But if you do agree with us, then you've got to stop him! It's too late for us to say anything.

JUSTIN Yeah, we can't tell him now. You have to try, at least.

DEVELOPING SPEAKING

3 Work in pairs. Discuss what happens next in the story. Write down your ideas.

We think Emma helps Liam by giving him some of her photos for the competition.

4 ▶️ **EP3** Watch to find out how the story continues.

5 Mark the statements T (true) or F (false).

1 Nicole talks to Liam but doesn't tell him what she really thinks. ☐

2 Liam thinks Emma really likes his photos. ☐

3 Nicole thinks Justin didn't try very hard. ☐

4 Emma, Justin, and Nicole decide to go to the photography exhibit separately. ☐

5 Justin claims that he had previously said that Liam was a great photographer. ☐

6 Liam took the winning photos with his phone. ☐

PHRASES FOR FLUENCY

1 Find these expressions in the photostory. Who says them? How do you say them in your language?

1 Anyway, … _____

2 Go for it! _____

3 … for starters! _____

4 get (his) hopes up _____

5 make a fool of (himself) _____

6 Fair enough. _____

2 Match the expressions in Exercise 1 to these meanings.

a try it ☐

b have high expectations ☐

c the first reason is … ☐

d appear ridiculous to others ☐

e I understand why you said / did that ☐

f So let me change the subject ☐

3 Use the expressions in Exercise 1, in the correct form, to complete the mini-dialogues.

1 A Well, there are lots of reasons I don't want to go there. It's very expensive, _____.

   B _____. We'll have to think of another place to go, then.

2 A There's a singing contest at school next month. I thought I might _____.

   B Well, don't _____; Nia's bound to win it.

3 A So, are you going to try out for the football team?

   B No, I decided not to. I'm not good enough, and I'd just _____.

   A Oh, no you wouldn't. Don't be so negative.

   B _____, even if I did get in, they play on Saturday morning, and I like to sleep in on Saturdays.

Workbook page 66

WordWise

SO

1 Look at these sentences about the photostory and video. Complete them with phrases from the list.

so far | I told you so | I'm afraid so
… or so | I guess so | So

1 JUSTIN _____.
   NICOLE You did not!

2 NICOLE _____, what are we going to do?

3 NICOLE Are the photos really that bad?
   JUSTIN _____.

4 LIAM It's amazing what great photos you can get just with your phone.
   EMMA Yes. Yes, _____.

5 LIAM I've only been taking photos for two months _____.

6 EMMA This is the best photo you've shown me _____.

2 Use expressions from Exercise 1 to complete the sentences.

1 A _____, have you decided what you want?
   B Not yet.

2 A Is it broken?
   B Yes, _____.

3 A How long does it take to get there?
   B Not long. Twenty minutes _____.

4 A How's it going?
   B OK. I've answered six questions _____. Only four more to do.

5 A Is Jack running late?
   B _____. He said he'd be here by now.

6 A This restaurant is horrible.
   B Well, _____, but you wouldn't listen!

Pronunciation

Intonation: encouraging someone

Go to page 121.

8 MAKING LISTS

READING

1 SPEAKING **Look at the photos. In pairs, think of:**

1 three ways in which the jobs are different
2 three things the jobs have in common
3 something that connects *all* of the pictures

Then compare your ideas with others in the class.

2 Read the book review quickly. What does Atul Gawande recommend using to ensure procedures are followed?

3 ◀)) 2.08 **Read the review again and listen. Match the paragraphs with the titles. There is one extra title.**

A Lives can be saved
B It's not just for the medical profession
C Mistakes don't really matter
D Holes in the system
E Not everyone agrees
F A book for everyone

4 Answer the questions.

1 What surprised the doctor who went into the operating room?
2 What was the result of an experiment in a large American hospital?
3 What examples does Gawande give of what could happen if engineers and pilots didn't follow checklists?
4 How did many of the doctors react to the idea of using checklists? Why do you think they reacted this way?
5 Why does the writer of the review recommend the book?

5 SPEAKING **Work in pairs. Discuss the questions.**

1 Can you think of any other jobs where checklists should be mandatory?
2 When have you made checklists for yourself? What for? Were they useful?
3 Do you agree with the last sentence in the review? Why or why not?

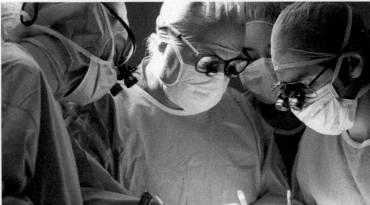

The Checklist Manifesto

by

Atul Gawande

Book of the month

1 A doctor in a large hospital walked into an operating room where an operation was being performed. Everything seemed to be going well, but the doctor noticed that no one was wearing a face mask. He was surprised – wearing a face mask is basic hospital procedure. But he didn't say anything. The operation was a success, but a few days later the patient came down with a fever. It turned out that she had contracted a serious infection, probably because the doctors and nurses hadn't followed a simple rule. If they'd worn their masks, the patient wouldn't have been infected.

2 Someone who'd be interested in that story is Atul Gawande, who wrote a book called *The Checklist Manifesto: How to Get Things Right*. Gawande is a doctor himself, and in his book he suggests that if surgeons run through a simple checklist before every operation, then lives will be saved. And he's got the numbers to prove it. In 2001, at a large American hospital, there was an experiment that required doctors to use a five-point checklist before they carried out specific procedures. The checklist was just a list of routine things doctors should normally do without thinking – wearing latex gloves, washing their hands before and after every patient, and so on. By making sure that the checklist was followed, there were almost no infections during the 27 months of the experiment, and they estimate that around eight lives were saved. When the checklist was tested again in hospitals in Michigan, infections went down by 66 percent.

3 In his book, Gawande looks at other professions, too, to support his argument that checklists reduce accidents and improve success rates. He points out that people like engineers and pilots use checklists all the time, and he comes up with some good examples. Just imagine that an airplane crashed because the pilot had failed to follow basic procedures. Suppose a skyscraper collapsed because the engineers hadn't remembered to do some important calculations. People would demand that officials look into these events immediately. So Gawande's question is: If pilots and engineers use checklists, why don't doctors use them?

4 When Gawande talked to doctors at eight hospitals about a checklist that he had developed, he found that a lot of them weren't very enthusiastic. Twenty percent of the doctors that Gawande talked to said the list would be too difficult to use and that it wouldn't help to save lives. But when they were shown the statement, "If I had surgery, I'd want the surgeon to use this list," 93 percent of the same doctors agreed with it! So it's hard to work out why they don't want to use it themselves.

5 *The Checklist Manifesto* is a really interesting and well-written book. It reminds us that sometimes the easiest way to avoid making mistakes is to follow a very simple set of rules. It's relevant for all of us, not just for doctors. We could all benefit from using checklists now and again.

■ TRAIN TO THiNK ■

The "goal-setting" checklist

When you take a trip, you don't say to yourself, "I don't know where I'm going, but I'll go anyway." How would you know if the place you end up is actually the place you want to be if you don't have a destination, a goal, in mind? This question applies to all our journeys in life. Having a goal-setting checklist can help you think clearly about what it is you want to achieve and how you're going to achieve it.

1 Martin has a new project. He wants to learn to play the guitar. Look at these ideas that Martin has written (a–h) and match them to the categories (1–5) below. (Some include more than one idea, and some could go in more than one category.)

a I'll be able to play about 20 songs _____
b approach it as something to be enjoyed _____
c I'll feel really good about my achievement _____
d learn to play the guitar _____

e positive comments from family and friends _____
f a friend who will teach me _____
g discipline to practice daily _____
h lessons streamed from the Internet _____

2 SPEAKING Think of something you want to achieve. Create a checklist to help you define your goals more clearly. Compare with a partner.

1 What I want to achieve
2 Things I need in order to achieve this goal
3 How I need to act or behave in order to achieve this goal
4 Things that tell me I have achieved this goal
5 Results of achieving goal for myself and others

GRAMMAR

Conditionals (review)

1   **Write the correct form of the verbs in parentheses and then check your answers in the book review on page 75. Then complete the table.**

1   If surgeons _____ (run) through a simple checklist before every operation, then lives _____ (be) saved.

2   If they _____ (wear) their masks, the patient _____ (not be) infected.

3   If pilots and engineers _____ (use) checklists, why _____ doctors _____ (use) them?

4   If I _____ (have) surgery, I _____ (want) the surgeon to use this list.

RULE:

Type of conditional	Example sentence	If clause	Main clause
Zero	0 __3__	simple present	1 _____
First	2 _____	3 _____	4 _____
Second	5 _____	6 _____	would(n't) + infinitive
Third	7 _____	past perfect	8 _____

2   **Match the four sentences a doctor might say to a patient with the situations a–d.**

1   If people take this medicine, they don't get headaches. ☐

2   If you take this medicine, you won't get headaches. ☐

3   If you took this medicine, you wouldn't get headaches. ☐

4   If you had taken this medicine, you wouldn't have gotten headaches. ☐

a   The patient didn't take the medicine.

b   The doctor is telling the patient a general fact about the medicine.

c   The patient isn't taking the medicine and gets headaches.

d   The doctor is telling the patient about a future result of taking the medicine.

3   **Write conditional sentences in your notebook.**

1   Reading books is a great idea. (0 conditional)
If you / read books, you / learn things about life.

2   I think you should buy the book. (1st conditional)
You / discover interesting things about pilots and doctors if you / read it.

3   Gawande's a doctor. (2nd conditional)
If Gawande / not be a doctor, he / not understand so much about this.

4   I read this book a week or two ago. (3rd conditional)
I / not find out about the importance of checklists if I / not read it.

Workbook page 72

VOCABULARY

Phrasal verbs (2)

1   **Use the phrases in the list to complete the sentences. Then check your answers in the book review on page 75.**

run through | points out | look into | carried out
came down with | comes up with | turned out

1   The patient _____ a fever.

2   It _____ that she had a serious infection.

3   If surgeons _____ a simple checklist before every operation, then lives will be saved.

4   Doctors used a five-point checklist before they _____ specific procedures.

5   He _____ that people like engineers and pilots use checklists all the time.

6   He _____ some good examples.

7   People would immediatley demand that officials _____ these events.

2   **SPEAKING** **Work in pairs. Discuss the meaning of the phrasal verbs in Exercise 1.**

3   **Use the correct form of one of the verbs in Exercise 1 to complete each sentence.**

1   The police are _____ why the accident happened.

2   My sister didn't go to school last week. She _____ a very bad cold.

3   The doctors _____ some tests to see what was wrong with me.

4   I'd like to _____ that the capital of Brazil isn't São Paulo; it's Brasilia.

5   Let's _____ the names to make sure we haven't forgotten anyone.

6   For many years I thought Max was French, but it _____ he's Canadian.

7   I tried to think of some ideas for the weekend, but I didn't _____ any good ones.

Workbook page 74

LISTENING

Why do we make lists?

1 SPEAKING Work in pairs. Look at these lists and discuss the questions.

    1 What's the purpose of each list?

    2 Why do people make lists like these?

2 ◀》2.09 Listen to an interview with a social psychologist. Which of the reasons for lists that you gave in Exercise 1 does she mention?

3 ◀》2.09 Listen again and complete the information. Use one or two words to complete the spaces.

Five reasons for making lists:

1 to _____ information

2 to aid your _____

3 to _____ ourselves

4 to decrease _____

5 to make you _____ about yourself

4 SPEAKING Match the lists in Exercise 1 to some of the reasons in Exercise 3. Compare your ideas with a partner.

5 SPEAKING Which of these kinds of lists do you make? Do you agree with the psychologist about why you make them?

A
eggs
apples
vegetables
chicken
salt

B
Best cities to study abroad
Tokyo
New York
London
Cape Town
Rio de Janeiro

C
Top five action films of all time
Die Hard
Insurgent
X-Men
The Bourne Identity
Mission Impossible

D
ask Suzanna to bring music
send out invitations
decorate the living room (balloons?)
ask Mom about food
new shoes!!

GRAMMAR

Mixed conditionals

1 ◀》2.10 Complete the sentences from the interview with the words or phrases in the list. Listen and check.

had | were | would have | would

1 If I _____ more organized, I _____ made a list.

2 If I _____ made a list, then I _____ know what to buy.

2 Look at the sentences again. Find the second and third conditional parts in each one. Then match them to the sentences in the rule.

> **RULE:** Sometimes we mix second and third conditional forms so that we can connect present and past actions.
> - To talk about the present result of an unreal or imagined past action, we use: *if + had +* past participle, *would ('d) +* verb. Sentence _____
> - To talk about the past result of an unreal or hypothetical present situation or fact, we use: *if +* simple past, *would ('d) have +* past participle. Sentence _____

3 Write mixed conditional sentences to describe these situations.

0 I don't have any money. I didn't buy that phone.
If I had some money, I'd have bought that phone.

1 Anna and Dan had a big argument. They aren't talking to each other.

2 We didn't leave early. That's why we're late now.

3 I don't have a good memory. I forgot her birthday.

4 I didn't eat breakfast. Now I'm hungry.

5 He didn't listen to the explanation. He can't do the homework.

4 Work in pairs. How many different mixed conditional examples can you make in two minutes?

If I was _____, I would have _____.

Workbook page 73

> ### Pronunciation
> **Weak forms with past modals**
> **Go to page 121.**

READING

1 **SPEAKING** What "top ten" lists have you seen (or written) recently? Tell a partner.

2 **Read the blog. Answer the questions.**

  1 Why is Andrew posting his own list this week?

  2 Where can you see the complete lists?

  3 What does Andrew want his readers to do?

ANDREW'S LIST BLOG

As you know, every week I post a top ten list here that someone has sent me. Well, this week, no one sent me anything, so I'm offering you a top ten list of ... my favorite top ten lists! And here they are.

1 Top ten uses for a potato
This isn't about cooking potatoes; it's about using them for things like making electricity or improving your skin!

2 Top ten strange museums
Here are some really weird museums you can visit (as long as you have the money to travel all over the world, of course).

3 Top ten worst countries at soccer
If you're into soccer, you might like this list, unless you're from somewhere like San Marino or American Samoa (they're on the list).

4 Top ten ugly creatures
There are some great photos here that I'm sure you'll love, provided you like seriously ugly fish and animals!

5 Top ten bad science fiction films
Imagine spending a whole weekend watching really bad sci-fi movies. My favorite is *Plan 9 from Outer Space*.

6 Top ten actors who don't like watching their own movies
Apparently Johnny Depp avoids viewing his own movies. He prefers to walk away with the experience of having made the movie rather than focusing on the end product – and he's not alone.

7 Top ten unexplained mysteries
Surprisingly, the Nazca lines in Peru and the Easter Island statues do not appear on this list, but there are ten other really strange mysteries from around the world.

8 Top ten stupid criminals
The bank robber who wrote, "Give me the money!" on an envelope with his name and address on it! He's just one of the hopeless criminals on this great list.

9 Top ten weird world records
What's the world record for the number of T-shirts being worn by one person at one time? And more things like that. (The answer, by the way, is 245.)

10 Top ten signs in bad English
Suppose you were in another country and saw a sign in a store that said, "Wee spik Inglish hear." You'd laugh out loud! If you like that kind of thing, you'll love this list!

So that's it for this week. You can access these lists by clicking on the titles, or go to the Archive page. Lastly – please send me a list, people; otherwise, I won't have anything for next week.

3 **Which list do each of these sentences come from? Write a number (1–10) in the boxes.**

  a The dog with the longest ears is Tigger – his ears are each about 30 centimeters long.

  b This place, in Avanos, Turkey, has a huge collection of hair from over 16,000 people – and it's all in a small cave.

  c If you cut one in half and rub it on your shoes, your shoes will look great.

  d There are some beautiful animals in Africa – but the warthog isn't one of them!

  e Near the bottom of the list are the Turks and Caicos Islands, where cricket is much more popular.

4 **SPEAKING** Which five lists would you like to read in full? Compare your ideas with a partner.

5 **SPEAKING** Choose one of these sentence stems, add a word or words at the end, and make a list. Or make a different list altogether. Write your list and then discuss with the class.

My top five most interesting ...
My top five worst ...
My top five strangest ...
My top five funniest ...

■ THiNK VALUES ■

Lists

1 **Check the sentences you agree with.**

☐ 1 I never waste my time reading top ten lists.

☐ 2 Top ten lists aren't meant to be taken seriously – just enjoy them!

☐ 3 Some top ten lists can be very useful.

☐ 4 People who write top ten lists must have very high opinions of themselves.

2 **SPEAKING** **Compare your choices with others in the class.**

3 **Which of these top ten lists would interest you? Put a check (✓) or an X (✗). Add one more thing of your own that you think would make for an interesting top ten list.**

1 someone's favorite songs ☐

2 things to do on the weekend in your town ☐

3 books to read ☐

4 things to do before you're 25 ☐

5 ways to make money ☐

6 things to do to relax and be happy ☐

7 _____ ☐

VOCABULARY

Alternatives to *if*: *suppose, provided, as long as, otherwise, unless*

> **LOOK!**
> - to hypothesize about the present: *suppose* + simple past, *would* + verb
> - to talk about a future possibility and its results: *as long as* / *unless* + simple present, *will* + verb

1 **Match the sentence halves about the blog.**

1 **Suppose** you were in another country and saw this sign in a store ☐

2 You can visit these museums, ☐

3 You might like this list, ☐

4 I'll post your list, ☐

5 Please send me a list, people; ☐

a **provided** it hasn't been done before.

b **as long as** you have the money to travel.

c – you'd laugh out loud.

d **otherwise**, I won't have anything for next week.

e **unless** you're from San Marino or American Samoa.

2 **Which of the words in bold in Exercise 1 means:**

1 but only if *as long as* / _____

2 imagine _____

3 if … not … _____

4 because if not _____

3 **Choose the correct options.**

1 I don't mind going to the movies alone *unless* / *provided* / *otherwise* it's something I really want to see.

2 I think I should go home now; *unless* / *provided* / *otherwise*, my parents will be worried.

3 You'll do fine on your test *unless* / *provided* / *suppose* you study enough.

4 I'll never speak to you again *otherwise* / *unless* / *provided* you say you're sorry right now!

5 OK, I'll tell you what happened, *as long as* / *suppose* / *unless* you promise not to tell anyone else!

6 *Suppose* / *Provided* / *Unless* we didn't have school today. What would you want to do?

Workbook page 74

FUNCTIONS

Qualifying a response

1 **Work in pairs. Read the sentences and discuss who is talking to whom and what they are talking about.**

1 You can borrow it if you drive really carefully. (as long as)

2 Yes, you can go to the party, if you promise to be home by 11 o'clock. (provided)

3 If you don't help me, I'll get really bad grades. (unless)

4 I'll fix it if you let me play games on it. (as long as)

5 Close the door, or it'll get cold in here. (otherwise)

6 Yes, you can practice if you don't make a lot of noise. (provided)

7 Imagine you could play the guitar. What kind of music would you play? (suppose)

2 **Now rewrite the sentences in Exercise 1 in your notebook using the words in parentheses.**

3 **A friend asks you these things. For each one, how would you qualify your response? Make notes.**

1 Can I use your phone to make a call?
   no international phone calls / no long phone calls

2 Will you come shopping with me?

3 Please come to the game with me.

4 Can I borrow your jacket, please?

4 **SPEAKING** **Use your notes in Exercise 3. Write your answers. Then work with a partner and act out the conversations for the situations.**

> Yes, all right – as long as / provided you don't make any international calls on it.

Culture

1 Centuries ago people created a list of the "Seven Wonders of the Ancient World." Do you know about any of the things or places on that list?

2 🔊 2.13 Read and listen to the article about the New Seven Wonders of the World. Which one is:

- the oldest? _____
- the newest? _____

The New Seven Wonders of the World

Recently, an online poll was held to choose the New Seven Wonders of the World. More than 100 million people voted. Here are the seven winners, in alphabetical order.

Chichén Itzá, Yucatan Peninsula, Mexico

This was an important city for the Mayans between about 800 and 1200 CE. A symbol of Mayan civilization, it was a center for trade in things like cloth, honey, and salt. Most photographs of Chichén Itzá show a 24-meter high pyramid called *El Castillo*. There is also a ruin known as *El Caracol*, which the Mayans used as an observatory – the view of the night sky from the top is beautiful.

Christ the Redeemer, Rio de Janeiro, Brazil

Built between 1922 and 1931, the *Cristo Redentor* statue on Mount Corcovado has become a worldwide icon of Brazil. Constructed of concrete and soapstone, the statue is about 30 meters high (and stands on an eight-meter-high pedestal). The outstretched arms measure 28 meters end to end. Designed by a Frenchman and built by Heitor da Silva Costa, it attracts thousands of visitors every year.

The Colosseum, Rome, Italy

This famous amphitheater, built between 70 and 80 CE, was used by the Romans for about 500 years for all kinds of public spectacles. Now it is almost a complete ruin as a result of earthquakes and the passage of time, but some parts can still be visited. The Colosseum has become one of the most famous images of Italy.

The Great Wall, China

This amazing structure was built over a period of more than 2,000 years, ending in the 16th century. It was built in order to keep out the hostile tribes of Mongolia on the other side. The Great Wall is not actually just one continuous wall, but a succession of many different ones. At 6,500 kilometers, it's the longest man-made structure on the planet.

Machu Picchu, Peru

Sitting high up in the Andes, the Inca city of Machu Picchu is believed to have been a sacred place for the inhabitants of nearby Cusco. The Incas built it in the mid-1400s, though we don't really know how. The Incas abandoned the city, and for many years only local people knew about it. It was rediscovered in 1911. Many tourists go there, mostly by train from Cusco.

Petra, Jordan

The city of Petra flourished from 9 BCE to 40 CE. It was the capital of the Nabataea Empire. The city was built in a desert area by the people of this civilization, who were very skilled at finding and storing water. Petra includes many buildings carved out of stone, an amphitheater that held 4,000 people, and a monastery. Petra became a World Heritage Site in 1985.

Taj Mahal, Agra, India

Built of white marble between 1632 and 1648, the world-famous Taj Mahal is thought of as one of the most beautiful buildings in the world. Its architecture is a mixture of Persian, Islamic, Turkish, and Indian styles. It was built by Emperor Shah Jahan as a place to bury his beloved wife, Mumtaz Mahal. Inside there are flower gardens and pools.

3 Read the article again. Which place or thing:

1. is in a desert?
2. has architecture from different places mixed together?
3. has been damaged by natural events?
4. was designed to protect the people who built it?
5. was built in ways we don't really understand?
6. took nine years to construct?
7. was used to look at the stars?

4 [VOCABULARY] **Match the highlighted words in the article to the definitions.**

1 left the place and never went back   _____
2 put something or someone into the ground   _____
3 grew, developed very successfully   _____
4 unfriendly and aggressive, wanting to attack   _____
5 a famous thing or person that represents a group or country   _____
6 exciting public shows or events   _____
7 one thing coming after another   _____
8 made by cutting   _____

WRITING

Essay

1 **Read Javed's essay on The Simplon Tunnel. Why does he think this is a modern wonder of the world?**

2 **Read the essay again. Ten things are underlined. Five of the things are mistakes; the other five are correct. Find an example of:**

- a spelling mistake
- a mistake with the verb tense
- a mistake with the wrong choice of connecting word
- a preposition mistake
- a mistake that is a missing word

3 **Correct the mistakes in Javed's writing.**

4 **Look again at the list of mistakes in Exercise 2.**

1 Are there other kinds of mistakes that people make in writing? What are they? (e.g., punctuation, ...)
2 Does the list in Exercise 2 show the kinds of mistakes that you have sometimes made in your writing? If you've made other kinds of mistakes, what were they?
3 Make a checklist for yourself: "Mistakes I should try not to make when I write in English."

5 **You're going to write an essay entitled "A Modern Wonder of the World."**

1 Look at question 2 in the Speaking exercise above. Choose one of the things that you discussed there.
2 Make notes about why you think this thing is a good choice for a modern wonder of the world.

6 **Write your essay in 150–200 words.**

- Make sure you state clearly what your choice is, and say where and what it is.
- Give reasons for your choice.
- When you have written your text, read it through again and use your checklist of personal mistakes (Exercise 4.3) to check for possible mistakes in your writing.

SPEAKING

Discuss in pairs or small groups.

1 Suppose you could visit one of the seven wonders. Which one would you choose and why?
2 Think of two things and/or places from your country that you could campaign to be included in a list of seven wonders of the world. Give reasons to support your choice.

A Modern Wonder of the World: The Simplon Tunnel

My choice for a modern wonder of the world is the Simplon Tunnel [1] at Switzerland. It's actually two tunnels – railway tracks run through both of them. They're each almost 20 kilometers long, so they're not [2] ... longest tunnels in the world now, but they were when they were built back in the beginning [3] of the twentieth century. The first one was started in 1898 and opened in 1906. The other one was started in 1912 and was opened in 1921, so each one [4] has taken about eight years to construct.

The first tunnel was built by drilling in both directions – when the two drill-holes met in 1905, they were only two centimeters out of alignment. In those days, that was a fantastic achievement.

While it [5] was being built, about 3,000 people worked on the construction every day. The working conditions weren't very good – for example, it was often very hot inside – and more than 60 people died [6] while the building of the tunnel.

The tunnel joins Switzerland and Italy, [7] and it has helped to make [8] ... travel between the two countries a lot easier [9] then it was before. Now, people can put their car on the train and take it through the tunnel, so they don't have to drive over the Simplon Pass.

I think this was a great thing to build all those years ago, and it has made a big difference to the [10] whole of that part of Europe.

READING AND USE OF ENGLISH
Part 2: Open cloze

Workbook page 71

1   For questions 1–8, read the text below and think of the word that best fits each space. Use only one word in each space. There is an example at the beginning (0).

Reasons to be cheerful

Despite ^{0} ___*what*___ you may hear on the news, the future is looking bright for teenagers. According to a government report, the economy is only months away ^{1}_____ making a dramatic recovery. And ^{2}_____ the report is correct, those who will benefit most are the young. In fact, it predicts that ^{3}_____ the time today's 13-year-olds finish school, unemployment will ^{4}_____ fallen to an all-time low. The report, which was carried ^{5}_____ by a leading employment agency, predicts that this growth will principally be in IT technology. It strongly recommends ^{6}_____ increase in the funding of science and technology and points out that failure to do this will mean that the U.S. will fall behind other countries. The message is clear: as ^{7}_____ as the country continues to take education seriously, tomorrow's graduates ^{8}_____ enjoy a prosperous future.

SPEAKING
Part 2: Individual long turn

Workbook page 79

2   Here are two photographs. They show different ways of making lists. Compare the photographs and say what the differences are and what you think are the main advantages of making lists in these ways.

VOCABULARY

1 **Complete the sentences with the words in the list. There are four extra words.**

about | flourishes | down | worried | up | dread | forward
as long as | through | worked | away | succession | unless | on

1 John had lots of problems, but he didn't let them get him _____ . He stayed cheerful.
2 Sally is excited. She's _____ to go paragliding for the first time.
3 When we were planning the trip, Leo came _____ with some good ideas.
4 Mom said we couldn't go to the concert _____ we got a taxi home because it'd be late.
5 He seems so down all the time. I'm really _____ about him.
6 My aunt is a great gardener. Everything she plants _____ .
7 The police are investigating a _____ of bank robberies.
8 The organizers wanted to run _____ the arrangements for the president's visit again.
9 I'm tired. I'm really looking _____ to my vacation.
10 Kate was seconds _____ from leaving the house when Mr. Hill phoned to cancel the meeting.

/10

GRAMMAR

2 **Complete the sentences with the words in the list. There are two extra words.**

won't | would be | would have | are going | will have | will | will be | don't

1 If Jenny had accepted the job offer, she _____ living in New York now.
2 By the end of the festival, I _____ seen about 15 movies.
3 Watch out! You _____ to hit that cyclist!
4 Don't stay on the computer all night, or you _____ feel exhausted the next day.
5 If I were taller, I _____ been chosen for the basketball team.
6 While my parents are away on vacation, I _____ looking after the dog.

3 **Find and correct the mistake in each sentence.**

1 It's Diana's birthday next Friday, and she will have a party on Saturday.
2 I would have been happy if he would have come.
3 If I hadn't made so many mistakes, I would win the tennis match.
4 This time tomorrow, I'm lying on a beach in the sun.
5 If I had been taller, I wouldn't need the ladder.
6 We must finish cleaning the kitchen before our parents are arriving.

/12

FUNCTIONAL LANGUAGE

4 **Choose the correct options.**

1 A Oh dear, I have *no / every* chance of saving enough money to fly to Mexico.
  B Come on, look on the *better / bright* side. If you don't, you can buy that new phone you want.
2 A Yes, you can use my computer *unless / provided* you finish before six o'clock.
  B That's fine! There's *any / a good* chance I'll only need it for half an hour.
3 A Mom won't let me watch the game *unless / as long as* I clean my room first.
  B Oh, *cheer / hang* up. Cleaning your room won't take long – I'll help you!
4 A Yes, you can borrow my video camera *if / as long* I can use your computer for a couple of hours.
  B OK, *as long / provided* as you don't spill anything on it.

/8

MY SCORE /30

| 22 – 30 |
| 10 – 21 |
| 0 – 9 |

9 BE YOUR OWN LIFE COACH

OBJECTIVES

FUNCTIONS: asking someone politely to change their behavior

GRAMMAR: *I wish* and *If only*; *I would prefer to, I would prefer it if / It's (about) time, I'd rather*

VOCABULARY: life's ups and downs; work and education

READING

1 Look at the photos. Match each thought to the people in the photos.

- [ ] "She doesn't understand me."
- [ ] "Why? Why? Why?"
- [ ] "I hate doing this."
- [ ] "I like it this way."

2 SPEAKING Work in pairs. Compare your answers from Exercise 1. Do you agree with each other? Then think of one piece of advice for each person to help them cope with life a little better.

3 Read the presentation quickly. Which of these titles is best in your opinion? Discuss your ideas with a partner.

You can change
Six steps to happiness
It's all in your mind

4 ◀) 2.14 Read the presentation again and listen. Match the paragraph headings with the paragraphs. There are two extras.

- A It's not always personal [ ]
- B Don't expect people to be perfect [ ]
- C You can't turn back the clock [ ]
- D Avoid exaggeration [ ]
- E Don't believe everything your friends tell you [ ]
- F Life isn't black and white [ ]
- G The truth is hard to accept [ ]
- H Don't let your emotions get the better of you [ ]

5 SPEAKING Work in pairs. Discuss the questions.

1 Which advice do you think is the best? Why? Which, if any, do you disagree with?

2 Which piece of advice would be the easiest to follow? Which would be the hardest?

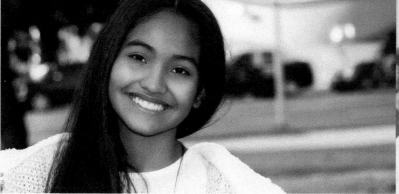

Life and how to live it

Life! It's a lot of fun, but it can also be challenging. Things don't always go our way. Life can let us down and can sometimes fail to deliver what we were hoping for. That's just the way it is. But sometimes the problems that trouble us are the ones that we create in our own minds. Maybe it's time to stop blaming other people, bad luck, the weather, our baseball team, or whatever, and look at ourselves. Here are a few simple tips we can use to instantly change the way we live for the better.

1. "My life's a mess. I just wish I could disappear." "Why do these things always happen to me?" "If only someone understood me." Thoughts like these help no one. Overdramatizing a situation only makes it worse. Try and put things into perspective a little, take a step back, sleep on it, ask a friend for help. Things are rarely as bad as they seem.

2. So your teacher didn't give you the part in the school play that you really wanted and had tried your hardest for at the audition. Well, that's a shame – things don't always work out the way we'd like them to, but it doesn't mean your teacher doesn't like you. Maybe there were other students who were better for the role. Likewise, when your baseball team loses, they don't lose just to upset you. Maybe they didn't play very well. Things go wrong for a million and one different reasons. It's not all about you.

3. Not all teachers are the enemy. Not all adults are clueless. Not all younger brothers and sisters are annoying. Try not to look at people so simplistically. Everyone is an individual. Open your mind to other possibilities. Get to know people as individuals – they might surprise you.

4. Do you sometimes snap at your parents just because they've asked you to clean up your room or do your homework? Just because you feel angry doesn't mean they're being unreasonable. Maybe you're tired or hungry. Maybe other problems with school or friends are getting in the way of you thinking clearly. Maybe you're overreacting. It's good to feel, but it's important to take a step back before you act on those feelings.

5. No one gets it right all of the time, and that includes you! So don't expect life to always work out the way you think it should. If others let you down, be kind to them. If you're not living up to your own expectations, be kind to yourself. If you're always looking for perfection in others, you're sure to be disappointed.

6. Don't dwell on the past. There's no point thinking, "If only I'd studied harder for that test," or, "I wish I hadn't said those things to my parents." You didn't study, and you failed. You said those things, and you got in trouble. There's nothing you can do to change any of that. Learn from it, and make sure you don't make the same mistakes again.

So there you go. Keep these tips in mind, and the next time life doesn't go exactly the way you want it to, try and use one or two. It's time to take control of your life.

■ TRAIN TO THiNK ■
Avoiding generalizations

People sometimes jump to conclusions with little evidence. Take Teresa, for example. She had an argument with a friend on the way to school. At school a teacher was not happy with her homework. When she got home, she had a fight with her mom. Five minutes later she was sitting in her room, thinking, "Everybody hates me." But of course, this isn't true. To spot generalizations, watch out for clue words such as all, none, always, everyone, never, no one, usually, hardly ever, practically every, *etc.*

1 **Read through these sentences. What are the generalizations in them? How do you know? How can you make them more accurate?**

   1 All Brazilians love soccer.
   2 Every teenager gets up late.
   3 It always rains on the weekend.
   4 Usually people who live in big cities are less caring than people who live in the countryside.
   5 Everyone loves a box of chocolates as a gift.
   6 Math is hard for practically everyone who is good at languages.

2 **SPEAKING** **Work in groups. Tell each other about some of the generalizations you have heard about teenagers.**

GRAMMAR
I wish and If only

1 **Complete the sentences with the correct form of the verbs in the list. Check in the presentation on page 85. Then complete the rule.**

understand | not say | can | study

1 I just wish I _____ disappear.
2 If only someone _____ me.
3 If only I _____ harder for that test.
4 I wish I _____ those things to my parents.

> **RULE:** To talk about how we would like things to be different now or in the future, we often use *I wish* or *If only* and the [1]_____ tense (Sentences 1 and 2).
> To talk about regrets we have about things we did in the past, we often use *I wish* or *If only* and the [2]_____ tense (Sentences 3 and 4).

2 **Complete the sentences using the verbs in parentheses.**

1 If only my parents _____ so angry with me all the time. They just don't understand me. (not get)
2 If only the teacher _____ my dad. He wouldn't be so angry with me now. (not tell)

VOCABULARY
Life's ups and downs

1 **Find the expressions in the presentation on page 85 and match them with their definitions.**

1 to (not) go your way ☐
2 to blame someone or something ☐
3 to let someone down ☐
4 to try your hardest ☐
5 to get in the way of something ☐
6 to dwell on something ☐
7 to (not) work out the way we'd like them to ☐
8 to (not) live up to your expectations ☐

a to disappoint someone
b to do your best
c to think about something for a long time (often meaning you can't make a decision about it)
d when the results of something are(n't) what we'd hoped for
e when the results are as good as you hoped or bad as you feared
f to say something is someone's fault
g to obstruct or prevent something
h when things happen (or not) the way you want them to

3 I wish I _____ up all night. I'm so tired now. (not stay)
4 Why does my soccer team always lose? If only we _____ occasionally. (win)
5 I wish our teacher _____ us so much homework today. I wanted to go out this evening, and now I can't. (not give)
6 If only I _____ to my parents. They wouldn't be so upset with me now. (not lie)
7 I wish my brother _____ with his mouth open. It's disgusting! (not eat)
8 I wish Annie _____ me to her party. Lots of my friends were invited. (invite)

3 **SPEAKING** **Look back at the people on pages 84 and 85. Write one wish for each person. Read the wish to a partner. Can he/she guess the photo?**

Workbook page 82 ➤

> ## Pronunciation
> ### The /tən/ word ending
> **Go to page 121.** 🔊

2 **Use the expressions in Exercise 1 in the correct form to complete the text.**

OK, so I made a mistake. I shouldn't have been playing soccer in the house. Now the window's broken – that's certainly going to [1]_____ my plans for a party this weekend. My parents are going to say I've [2]_____ them _____ and that I'm not responsible enough to be home by myself. Well, I didn't [3]_____ it for too long and decided to try and do something to make them proud. I decided to make dinner. I [4]_____ my _____, I really did, but things have [5]_____ well, and the baked chicken is pretty disappointing. It hasn't really [6]_____ to my _____. I mean, I thought it was going to be a beautiful golden brown color like in the book, but mine is black all over. I [7]_____ the oven. I think it's hotter than it says it is. And then the mashed potatoes. I mean how did they turn out so watery? Some days nothing seems to [8]_____ my _____. Oh well, the table looks nice. Although that candle does look kind of close to the curtains. Oh no! I need some help. Quick!

Workbook page 84 ➤

LISTENING

1 **SPEAKING** Work in pairs. Look at the photos of two 19-year-olds and discuss the questions.

1 What do they do?
2 How are their lives similar, and how are they different?
3 How do you imagine they feel about their future?

2 🔊 2.17 **Listen to a radio show. Which of the two life choices in the photos in Exercise 1 does Joe, a career counselor, recommend that Alex pursue next year?**

3 🔊 2.17 **Listen again and choose the correct answers.**

1 How many students who graduated from college last year found a job?

  A a quarter   B half   C three-quarters

2 What is the average cost of a four-year degree from a university?

  A $8,000
  B $18,000
  C $80,000

3 What does Joe think about young people's prospects?

  A They are very depressing.
  B There are many reasons to be optimistic.
  C They will have to do very well in school to get a good job.

4 Which one of these sentences is <u>not</u> mentioned in relation to Alex?

  A He feels pressure to go to college.
  B He's not smart enough to go to college.
  C He doesn't know what he wants to study.

5 What does Joe recommend to people in Alex's situation?

  A get some work experience before college
  B go on vacation before college
  C do what their friends are doing

6 What does Joe say is attractive to many employers?

  A employees with a good education
  B employees who can speak a foreign language
  C employees who have already done some useful things in their lives

VOCABULARY
Work and education

1 **Match the words and the definitions.**

1 work experience ☐
2 counselor ☐
3 higher education ☐
4 a degree ☐
5 a graduate ☐
6 life experience ☐
7 a major ☐

a practical wisdom gained from living
b experience of having a job
c someone's main course of study at a college or university
d someone who has recently finished school
e schooling after high school
f something a person earns by studying at a college or university
g someone who gives advice about work and educational choices

2 **Complete the paragraph using the words from Exercise 1 in the correct form. Use each term only once.**

I finish school in two years, but I'm already kind of worried about what I'm going to do. I would love to get some [1]_____, but there aren't a lot of good jobs for high school [2]_____, so I'll probably go straight into [3]_____. I'm not sure what to choose as my [4]_____, so I'm going to meet with a career [5]_____ first. Once I've got my [6]_____, I'm not sure I want to go straight into a career. It would be nice to take some time off and get some [7]_____ first.

SPEAKING

Read the sentences and write A (agree) or D (disagree). Discuss in small groups.

1 It's a good idea to get work experience while you're still in school. ☐
2 All students should see a career counselor before they graduate. ☐
3 Higher education isn't for everyone. ☐
4 It's important to have a college degree to be successful in life. ☐
5 A college education is too expensive. ☐

Workbook page 84 ▶

READING

1 Read the quiz from a teen magazine and choose your answers.

2 Compare your answers with a partner.

3 Now read the key. Do you agree with the advice? Do you think this is a fair description of you? Why or why not?

4 `SPEAKING` Work in pairs. The key suggests that C answers are always the best way to behave. Look at each of the questions again and decide if you agree with this. In which instances do you think A or B might be better? Why?

Mostly A's – Hmm. It seems that you're not really in control of life's little problems. Try not to be so aggressive when things don't go your way.

Mostly B's – You're not bad at dealing with life's little problems, but you still need to assert yourself and not always give in to what other people want.

Mostly C's – You are an expert at dealing with life's little problems. You know what you want and the best way to get it.

Are you in *control?*

It's not always easy to keep on top of things when there are so many little things in life that are out of your control. But when things aren't going your way, can you keep your head while everyone around you is losing theirs? Take our quiz and find out!

1 Your younger sister is practicing the guitar loudly in her bedroom. You're trying to study. What do you say to her?
- **A** Turn it off. Now!
- **B** I'd rather you didn't practice right now. I need to study.
- **C** Could I borrow your headphones?

2 Your best friend wants to play a football game on the computer. You'd prefer to go out and play a real game. What do you say to him?
- **A** OK.
- **B** I'd rather go to the park and play football for real.
- **C** How about we play on the computer for half an hour and then we go to the park and play?

3 It's the weekend, and you're sleeping late. Your dad's in a bad mood. He storms into your room and says, "It's about time you got out of bed and did something." What do you say?
- **A** Dad, I'm sleeping.
- **B** I'll be down in half an hour.
- **C** OK, Dad. What do you want me to do?

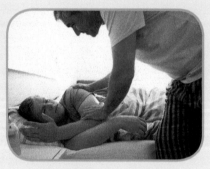

4 You got 60% on a test. How do you feel?
- **A** Really angry. Why didn't I get 70%?
- **B** That's OK, I suppose.
- **C** Oh well, I'll study harder for my next test.

5 Your sister or brother keeps borrowing your clothes without asking. What do you say?
- **A** I'm telling Mom.
- **B** I'd prefer it if you didn't keep taking my things.
- **C** If you want to borrow something, why don't you just ask?

6 You and your friend need to catch a bus that leaves in 30 minutes. Your friend wants to walk to the bus stop, but he isn't quite ready. It takes 20 minutes to get there. What do you say to him?
- **A** I'm not waiting for you. Bye.
- **B** I'd prefer to take a taxi, just to be on the safe side.
- **C** No problem as long as we leave in the next two minutes.

GRAMMAR
I would prefer to, I would prefer it if /
It's (about) time, I'd rather

1 Choose the correct option. Check your answers in the quiz. Then read the rule and match each point to the five sentences.

1 I'd rather you *don't / didn't* practice right now.

2 I'd rather *go / went* to the park and play football for real.

3 It's about time you *get / got* out of bed and did something.

4 I'd prefer it if you *don't / didn't* keep taking my things.

5 I'd prefer to *take / taking* a taxi.

> **RULE:** To say we think someone should do something, we can use:
> - *It's (about) time* + subject + simple past   sentence [1]_____
>
> To talk about our own preference, we can use:
> - *I'd rather* + base form of verb   sentence [2]_____
> - *I'd prefer* + infinitive   sentence [3]_____
>
> If the subject of the second verb is different from the subject of *'d rather / prefer*, we use:
> - *I'd rather* + subject + simple past   sentence [4]_____
> - *I'd prefer it if* + subject + simple past   sentence [5]_____

2 Complete the sentences with the correct form of the verbs in the list.

learn | leave | go | stay in | not tell
eat | not invite | play

1 I really don't like listening to opera in the car. I'd rather you _____ something else.

2 It's a secret. I'd prefer it if you _____ anyone else.

3 I'm tired. It's about time I _____ to bed.

4 I don't really like Tim. I'd rather you _____ him to the party.

5 We had Italian food last week. I'd rather _____ at a Chinese restaurant tonight.

6 I don't want to miss the train. I'd rather _____ the house a little earlier.

7 Can't you make yourself something to eat? It really is time you _____ to cook.

8 I don't really want to go out. I'd prefer _____ tonight.

> Workbook page 83 →

FUNCTIONS
Asking someone politely to change their behavior

1 Look at the picture and complete the conversation with an appropriate verb in the correct form.

MOM   Josh, I'd rather you [1]_____ your phone at the table.

JOSH   Sorry, Mom. I'll just be a second.

MOM   And I'd prefer you [2]_____ with your mouth open.

JOSH   I'll try not to.

MOM   And I'd prefer it if you [3]_____ your feet on the floor, not on the table.

JOSH   OK, Mom. Is there anything I *can* do?

MOM   Yes, you can improve your table manners!

2 Use the picture and the expressions in Exercise 1 to write a short conversation between the passenger and the driver.

■ THiNK SELF-ESTEEM ■
Being diplomatic

It's not always good to be entirely truthful, especially when you could hurt someone's feelings or cause an argument. In these cases, it's better to try and find a way of being "diplomatic" and to say something that won't be offensive.

SPEAKING Work in pairs. Decide the best way to handle each of these situations. What do you say in each one?

1 Your younger brother wants to watch TV, but your younger sister wants to play games on the TV. There's only one TV in the house. It's in the room where you're trying to study.

2 Your mom and dad have made plans for a family visit to your grandparents' this Saturday. They've forgotten that you have a school football game that day.

3 You're at a friend's house having dinner. They're having fish. You really don't like fish.

4 Your aunt gives you a really horrible sweater for your birthday. She made it herself. You politely say you love it, and she offers to make you another one.

Literature

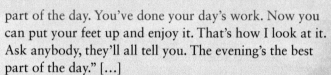

1   Look at the book cover. Then read the introduction to the extract. Do you think you would like to read the book? Why or why not?

The Remains of the Day
by Kazuo Ishiguro

Stevens has spent his life as a butler, working for Lord Darlington. He is now an elderly man. At the end of the book, he finds himself sitting alone on a bench, on a pier at the seaside. A stranger begins to talk to him, and Stevens starts to tell the man about his life and his feelings about Lord Darlington.

Y ou must have been very attached to this Lord whatever. And it's three years since he passed away, you say? I can see you were very attached to him, mate."

"Lord Darlington wasn't a bad man. He wasn't a bad man at all. And at least he had the privilege of being able to say at the end of his life that he made his own mistakes. His lordship was a courageous man. He chose a certain path in life, it proved to be a misguided one, but there, he chose it, he can say that at least. As for myself, I can't even claim that. You see, I trusted. I trusted in his lordship's wisdom. All those years I served him, I trusted I was doing something worthwhile. I can't even say I made my own mistakes. Really – one has to ask oneself – what dignity is there in that?"

"Now, look, mate, I'm not sure I follow everything you're saying. But if you ask me, your attitude's all wrong, see? Don't keep looking back all the time, you're bound to get depressed. And all right, you can't do your job as well as you used to. But it's the same for all of us, see? We've all got to put our feet up at some point. Look at me. Been happy as a lark since the day I retired. All right, so neither of us are exactly in our first flush of youth, but you've got to keep looking forward."

And I believe it was then that he said:

"You've got to enjoy yourself. The evening's the best part of the day. You've done your day's work. Now you can put your feet up and enjoy it. That's how I look at it. Ask anybody, they'll all tell you. The evening's the best part of the day." […]

It is now some twenty minutes since the man left, but I have remained here on this bench to await the event that has just taken place – namely, the switching on of the pier lights. As I say, the happiness with which the pleasure-seekers gathering on this pier greeted this small event would tend to vouch for the correctness of my companion's words; for a great many people, the evening is the most enjoyable part of the day. Perhaps, then, there is something to his advice that I should cease looking back so much, that I should adopt a more positive outlook and try to make the best of whatever remains of my day. After all, what can we ever gain in forever looking back and blaming ourselves if our lives have not turned out quite as we might have wished? […] What is the point in worrying oneself too much about what one could or could not have done to control the course one's life took? Surely it is enough that the likes of you and me at least try to make our small contribution count for something true and worthy. And if some of us are prepared to sacrifice much in life in order to pursue such aspirations, surely that is in itself, whatever the outcome, cause for pride and contentment.

---

2   **Read the extract quickly and choose the best ending for the statement.**

Stevens thinks that maybe he should stop …

a   talking to people he doesn't know.
b   thinking about the past so much.
c   going out in the evening.

3   🔊 2.18 **Read the extract again and listen. Correct these sentences by referring to the extract.**

1   Lord Darlington died five years ago.
2   Stevens thinks that Lord Darlington made the right decisions.
3   The stranger is a young man.
4   The people on the pier aren't happy when the lights come on.
5   Stevens thinks that it's useful to reflect on what he could have done better in his life.

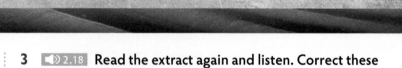

4 VOCABULARY Match the highlighted words in the extract with the definitions.

1 a feeling of self-respect or behavior that shows self-respect
2 people who are looking for fun
3 the time when you are young
4 an important male servant in a large house
5 feeling pleased with your situation and not wanting it to change or improve
6 not correct because it's based on wrong information or beliefs
7 the things you hope to achieve
8 support the idea that something is true or someone is honest

5 SPEAKING Work in pairs. Discuss the questions.

1 The man says: "Don't keep looking back all the time – you've got to keep looking forward." To what extent do you think he's right?

2 What part of the day do you like most? Why?

WRITING
A magazine article

1 Read Eve's article and answer the questions.

1 Does she agree with the statement?

2 What are her main arguments to support her position?

Students should try to get some work experience before they go to college

Do you really want to spend the rest of your life either studying or working? Wouldn't you like the chance to do a little more with your life and find out what it is you really want?

Most young people who choose to go to college go right after high school. A few may take a year or two off to travel or earn some money, but how many take five or six years or even longer before they go on to study more?

These days, young people are led to believe that the pressures in the labor market are so high that they cannot afford to waste any time doing things that won't directly help them get a good job. They feel that if they haven't graduated by the age of 22, they will be too old to be successful.

This is simply not true. Graduates are feeling the pressure precisely because so many of them are looking for the same jobs at the same time, and there's very little difference between them to help an employer make a decision.

Anyone who is brave enough to wait a few years before they go to college will, so long as they have used their time well, be far more attractive as an employee. Their extra life experience will mean they can offer companies so much more than any fresh-faced 22-year-old can. Besides, the fact they've taken time to decide exactly what they want to do shows that now they really want to do it.

So go on. Be brave. Delay. Go find out a little more about life. After all, you've got the rest of your life to work.

2 Look at the first and last paragraphs of the article. What technique does Eve use in each one? What effect does this have on the reader?

3 Choose one of the topics below. What is your position? What are your main arguments to support your position? Write notes.

- Going to college is a waste of money.
- The government should pay for all higher education.

My position	Argument 1	Argument 2	Argument 3

4 You're going to write an article for your school magazine about the topic you chose in Exercise 3. Think carefully about how to start and finish it.

1 Think of two direct questions you could use to start the article.

2 Think of two imperatives to conclude your article.

5 Write your article (200–250 words).

10 SPREADING THE NEWS

READING

1 Look at the photos. How are these people getting or giving news? Can you think of any other ways of giving or getting news?

2 Work in pairs. Match these opinions to the photos in Exercise 1. They can match more than one photo. Is each one an advantage or disadvantage?

1 *It takes forever.*

2 *You can read what you want, when you want.*

3 *You can only speak to someone if they're at home.*

4 *You can see how the other person reacts.*

5 *You have to be careful what you write.*

6 *You can't always get reception.*

3 **SPEAKING** Think of more advantages and disadvantages for each of the different ways of sharing news in Exercise 1. Compare with another pair.

4 ◀)) 2.19 Read and listen to the magazine article. What are three ways in which people use Twitter?

5 Read the Tweets. Which of the paragraphs in the article are they examples of? Write 1, 2, or 3.

1 Don't forget – my new single will be released tomorrow. ☐

2 We can stop animal cruelty here and now. Retweet this photo. ☐

3 I've just heard there was an earthquake in the capital! ☐

4 Government sources confirm the law has just passed. ☐

5 Yesterday's concert was great. Thanks Bruno Mars – you rock! ☐

6 We're meeting to protest outside the town hall tonight. Be there! ☐

6 **SPEAKING** Work in pairs. Discuss the questions.

1 What's the most reliable way to get accurate news? Give reasons. How often do you use that source?

2 Do you always believe what people tweet? How do you verify important information that comes to you via social media?

3 Is Twitter more about being informed or being entertained? Give reasons.

Everybody's Tweeting

When Twitter co-founder Jack Dorsey posted his first Tweet on his newly-created website, even he couldn't have imagined that just a few years later over 200,000,000 people would be doing the same thing at least once a month. With the words "just setting up my twttr," Jack launched a site that would change how we communicate forever.

Twitter was originally created as a messaging system for a podcasting website, but it took on a life of its own as people realized it offered them the power to connect with millions of people instantly. Suddenly everyone had a voice, as long as it could be shared in no more than 140 characters. But how well are we all using it, and just how is Twitter changing the way we do things?

> Oh no! I just heard about Robin Williams – so sad.   Astor, 16

1 Perhaps the greatest impact Twitter has had is on breaking news. Before Twitter, news had to get the attention of a journalist, who then had to make sure the news was accurate and true before finally broadcasting it on the radio or TV. These days anyone who happens to be in the right place at the right time with a Twitter account can post the news the second it happens. With retweets it can be halfway around the world in seconds. A dramatic example of this was when a U.S. flight made an emergency landing in the Hudson River in New York City. "There's a plane in the Hudson. I'm on the ferry going to pick up the people. Crazy," is how eyewitness Janis Krums broke the story to the world with this Tweet and a photo of the extraordinary event.

2 Young people have always loved to follow the activities of celebrities, and Twitter has made it a whole lot easier. Before the Internet, teenagers used to join the fan clubs of their favorite bands and write letters to their heroes. If they were lucky, two weeks later they'd get a reply written by a club secretary. A few times a year they'd receive a magazine updating them on all the band's "news." Today's teenagers don't need to wait. By following their idols on Twitter they get all the news the minute it happens. They get to hear what they had for breakfast, what they did the night before, what they're thinking as they sit waiting for a plane, and what they're going to do the next day. And they get to hear it directly from the people themselves.

> OMG I just saw Ariana Grande downtown. Can't wait for the concert tonight.   Rita, 14

3 Twitter allows people who think the same way to get together and do something about the things they care about. They can share information, organize campaigns, and put pressure on governments and big businesses to change. It allows people to stand up to things such as cyber bullying, sexism, and racism. Twitter has given the ordinary man and woman on the street the power to make a difference.

> Save our movie theater. Join us tonight 8 p.m. outside the mayor's house.   Dylan, 17

◼ TRAIN TO THINK ◼

Identifying the source of a piece of news

It's good to get an idea of the background of a person who says or writes something. Are they an impartial expert, or are they someone who wants to change your opinion to suit their own agenda? Consider this statement about a flu epidemic: "We need to be aware that patients can spread the virus a day before they show symptoms." This is more likely to come from a doctor than a politician. On the other hand, "We have to stop people with this virus from entering our country" is more likely from a politician. If you know the source of information, you're better able to decide how much importance to give it and whether you can really trust what they say.

Read these statements about Twitter. Match them with the person you think said them. Which do you think is the least trustworthy? Why?

1 a psychologist | 2 a politician | 3 a linguist
4 an IT expert | 5 an advertising executive

a We have noticed that people use fewer abbreviations on Twitter than in texting, and Tweets seem to show more creative word use.   □

b Young people sometimes make things public that they regret later. This can cause emotional problems and frequently a feeling of helplessness.   □

c We're trying to develop a system that will help people to upload multiple photos faster.   □

d We use social media in order to spread our key messages more efficiently.   □

e Twitter – quite simply the most effective way to reach our target consumers.   □

GRAMMAR
Reported speech (review)

1 **Read these examples of reported speech and rewrite them in direct speech using "I." Compare what you have written with the Tweets on page 93. Then complete the rule.**

1 She said that she had just heard about Robin Williams and that she was sad.

2 She said that she had just seen Ariana Grande downtown and that she couldn't wait for the concert that night.

3 He said they should save their movie theater and told people to join them that night at 8 p.m. outside the mayor's house.

> **RULE:** When we report what someone said, we often change the verb tense.
>
> simple present → *simple past*
> present continuous → 1 _____
> present perfect → 2 _____
> simple past → 3 _____
> will → 4 _____
> can → 5 _____
>
> We also change certain other words.
>
> here → *there*
> now → 6 _____
> this → 7 _____
> today → 8 _____
> tomorrow → 9 _____
> yesterday → 10 _____
> tonight → 11 _____
>
> Don't forget to change any pronouns so that they agree with any subject changes, e.g., *my → his/her*.

2 **Report these Tweets that you've received.**

1 I'll be in town later this evening.
   He _____.

2 We had a great time at your house yesterday. Thanks.
   They _____.

3 I miss you. I can't wait for tomorrow!
   She _____.

4 John's missed his train. He's going to be late.
   John's mom _____.

5 The baby's due today!
   Silvio _____.

3 **Write four Tweets about your day and plans for the future for your partner to report.**

Workbook page 90

VOCABULARY
Sharing news

1 **Match the phrases with their meanings.**

1 I'll <u>let you know</u> as soon as I hear anything. ☐

2 If you see Jim, can you <u>pass along the message</u>? ☐

3 An old friend of mine <u>got in touch</u> with me on Facebook the other day. ☐

4 It's so easy to <u>keep in touch</u> with all your friends these days. ☐

5 When you tell her, <u>break the news</u> gently. ☐

6 His followers <u>retweeted</u> his message more than 10,000 times. ☐

7 I'll <u>forward</u> you the details. ☐

8 <u>Give me a call</u> when you get home. ☐

a tell him   e stay in contact
b phone me   f sent on (via Twitter)
c tell you   g send on (via email or text)
d made contact   h tell her what's happened

2 **Using the phrases from Exercise 1 complete the questions with the missing verbs, in the correct form.**

1 If you're going to be home late, how do you _____ your parents know?

2 How do you prefer to _____ information to other people?

3 Do you _____ in touch with any of your friends from elementary school?

4 What's the best way to _____ in touch with people from your past?

5 What's the best way to _____ bad news?

6 Have you ever _____ someone else's message on Twitter?

7 What's the easiest way to _____ someone's contact information to others, by email or text?

8 Do you always _____ your best friend a call on their birthday? I usually send them a text.

3 **SPEAKING** **Work in pairs. Discuss the questions in Exercise 2.**

> I usually send them a text.

Workbook page 92

Pronunciation

Linking: omission of the /h/ sound
Go to page 121.

LISTENING

1 You are going to listen to an interview with Daniella Alvarez, a foreign correspondent. What do you think her job involves?

2 🔊 2.22 Daniella is being interviewed about her work by a group of students at a job fair. Listen to the interview and mark the sentences T (true) or F (false).

1 A lot of the time, Daniella is not at home. ☐

2 Her work is always dangerous. ☐

3 Sometimes, she would prefer to be a reporter in an office. ☐

4 Sometimes she needs to be physically fit. ☐

5 Sometimes her reports upset local governments. ☐

6 She thinks she is lucky to have her job. ☐

3 🔊 2.22 Listen again and answer the questions in your notebook.

1 What does a correspondent have to do to get a really good story?

2 How does Daniella rely on the help of local people in her work?

3 What does she sometimes have to do in order to stay in shape?

4 She mentions one thing she didn't enjoy. What was it?

5 Why did she once have to leave a country?

4 SPEAKING Work in pairs. Discuss the questions.

1 Would you like to be a foreign correspondent? Why or why not?

2 Which place(s) do you think would be the most difficult for Daniella to go to right now? Why?

GRAMMAR

Reported questions and requests

1 Here are three sentences from the interview with Daniella Alvarez. Which are questions, and which are requests? Write the direct questions, and complete the rule with *requests*, *yes/no questions*, or *wh- questions*.

1 You asked me if my job was dangerous.

a "Is _____?"

2 She asked me to share a story.

b "Can _____ of that?"

3 Just now, someone asked me why I do [this job].

c "Why _____?"

> **RULE:** In reported [1]_____ we use *if* or *whether* and the same word order as in a statement.
> In reported [2]_____ we use the question word and the same word order as in a statement. We do not use auxiliaries.
> In reported [3]_____ we use *asked* + person + infinitive.

2 Here are more questions the students asked Daniella Alvarez. Put them into reported speech. Be careful with the word order.

0 "When did you start your job?"

A student asked her when she had started her job.

1 "Which newspaper do you work for?"

2 "Where are you going next?"

3 "Have you ever been scared in your job?"

4 "Is your job well-paid?"

5 "Who is your boss?"

Workbook page 91

SPEAKING

1 Work in groups of four. Imagine you are journalists. You are going to interview well-known people you have never met before. Agree together on four people. For each person, write four or five questions to ask them.

2 Act out the interviews: One of you is the well-known person; the others ask the questions and write down the answers.

3 Each group reports to the class about the group's interviews.

> *We talked to [famous singer].*
> *We asked him when he started singing.*
> *He said he had always sung …*

WRITING

A magazine article

Write a magazine article about your interview. Make sure you:

- give a short introduction to the person
- say why you chose this person
- include reported questions and statements

Write your article (140–190 words).

READING

1 Read the magazine article and match each section with a heading.

a ☐ Breaking the law
b ☐ Just leave them alone
c ☐ It's a trap

2 Answer the questions.

1 What were journalists investigating about the supermarket?
2 What tools did the journalists use to get their information?
3 How did the newspaper editor use the information from the phone messages?
4 Why did the judge give the editor a prison sentence?
5 Why did Amy Winehouse go to court?
6 What was the judge's decision in the Amy Winehouse case?

BAD NEWS

Journalists are essential to tell us what is happening in the world, and with this comes a lot of responsibility. Journalists need to be able to report the facts without bias or prejudice and use only ethical means to obtain these facts. Unfortunately, not every journalist always does this.

1 Undercover operations are one of the most controversial ways a journalist can get a story. A reporter pretends to be a different person and goes "under cover" in a situation to find out something about a group or a corporation. In 1992 two TV journalists got jobs at a large U.S. supermarket. They were investigating the safety of the food sold there. They wore wigs with hidden microphones and cameras. At their "jobs," the reporters saw the store selling spoiled meat. When they published their story, the supermarket *accused* the journalists of lying and took them to court. But the supermarket didn't say the journalists had lied about the story. They said they had lied about being different people.

The journalists *admitted* to lying to get the jobs, but *denied* having done anything wrong.

2 Whereas undercover operations might be legal, everyone *agrees* that phone-hacking is certainly not. In 2007 the editor of a leading U.K. newspaper was sent to prison because he and a private detective had hacked into hundreds of voicemail messages of people who worked for the British royal family. The information they got was used in newspaper stories about members of the royal family.

The men also admitted to having taken messages from the phones of models, politicians, and athletes.

Although the editor said he *regretted* having invaded the privacy of these people and *apologized* for causing his victims distress, the judge sentenced him to four months in prison, explaining that newspaper editors had to obey the law as well. He *warned* other journalists not to make the same mistake.

Since then, however, many celebrities such as Jude Law and Sienna Miller have been subjected to illegal phone-hacking by journalists.

3 The paparazzi are famous for pursuing the rich and famous, hoping to get a photograph to sell to media outlets. In the last years of her life, singer Amy Winehouse was followed by photographers everywhere she went – and it got so bad that in 2009 she went to court and asked a judge to stop them. Her management team complained that her safety had been compromised because of so much attention from newspapers and magazines.

The judge *criticized* the journalists for behaving so badly and *agreed* to help her. He *ordered* the photographers to stay away from her home, saying that they could not come within 100 meters of Winehouse's new home. Many other celebrities have needed to obtain similar court orders to protect themselves and their families.

SPEAKING

Work in pairs. Discuss the questions.

1 Which of the journalistic methods mentioned in the text are acceptable and, which aren't, in your opinion? Give reasons.
2 Is it OK for a journalist to lie to get information for a story?
3 What do you think is the difference between reporters and the paparazzi? Do reporters and celebrity photographers sometimes cross the line and go too far? Give an example.

VOCABULARY
Reporting verbs

1 Complete the examples with the missing verbs, using the article on page 96 to help you. Then read and complete the rule with the missing verbs.

admitted | apologized | regretted | warned
accused | denied | criticized | agrees | ordered

1 The supermarket _____ the journalists of lying.
2 The journalists _____ to lying to get the jobs.
3 They _____ having done anything wrong.
4 Everyone _____ that phone-hacking is not.
5 The editor said he _____ having invaded the privacy of these people.
6 He _____ for causing his victims distress.
7 The judge _____ other journalists not to make the same mistake.
8 The judge _____ the journalists for behaving so badly.
9 He _____ the photographers to stay away from her home.

RULE: Different reporting verbs are followed by different verb patterns. Here are some of the more common ones.

pattern	examples
+ [person] + of + gerund	accuse
+ for gerund	1 _____
+ infinitive / that clause	2 _____
+ gerund or that clause	admit / 3 _____ / regret
+ to + gerund	admit
+ [person] + infinitive	4 _____
+ [person] + infinitive / about	warn
+ [person] for gerund	5 _____

2 Report these sentences using the verb given.

0 It was me. I took your sandwich. (admit)
   He admitted taking her sandwich.
1 I didn't do it. I didn't steal the money. (deny)
2 You did it. You told Jim my secret! (accuse)
3 Don't touch that dog. It bites! (warn)
4 I wish I hadn't said those things. I really do. (regret)
5 I'm really sorry I broke your phone. (apologize)
6 You drive so badly. Can't you slow down? (criticize)
7 Sure, I'll take you to the party. (agree)
8 Clean up your room. Now! (order)

Workbook page 92

FUNCTIONS
Making a point

1 ◁))2.23 Read the potential news story below. Listen to two different newspaper editors saying what they think about it. Which editor wants to run the story? Listen again. How do the editors justify their views? Who do you agree with?

A woman, who was once on a reality TV show and has kept her name in the paper ever since by saying outrageous things, has caused controversy again by tweeting something rude about the president.

2 ◁))2.23 Put the words in order to make sentences. Then listen again and check.

1 news / way / There's / story / this / is / no / a
2 story / really / running / against / I'm / this
3 up / My / made / mind's
4 want / is / exactly / of / This / the / kind / story / we
5 definitely / We're / with / story / going / this
6 final / that's / And

■ THiNK VALUES ■

News or not?

1 SPEAKING Work in pairs. You are the editors of a newspaper. For each of the stories below, decide if you would publish the story or not. Give your reasons.

☐ A famous singer and her husband seem to be having problems with their marriage. They were videoed having an argument in a restaurant. She walked out, leaving her husband on his own.

☐ A politician accepted $150,000 from a businessman who wanted his help to get his controversial building plans approved. The businessman was really a newspaper reporter who secretly recorded the whole thing.

☐ A 15-year-old boy has planned to ride his bike 500 kilometers from his hometown to Chicago to raise money for his brother, who is suffering from a rare illness.

☐ A plane that had just taken off from Memphis had to return when one of the passengers on board became angry and tried to open the emergency exit.

☐ A top doctor has said that unless his hospital charges more money, they will be unable to help everyone who needs hospital care.

2 SPEAKING Work with another pair and come to an agreement about which two of the above five stories to feature on your front page.

The news clip

1 Look at the photos and answer the questions.

1 Where do you think the four friends are going?

2 Why do you think Nicole's late for the bus?

2 ◆)2.24 Now read and listen to the photostory. Check your ideas.

JUSTIN Where is Nicole? We're going to miss the bus.

EMMA We've still got a few minutes. She'll be here. She wouldn't miss a trip to the skateboard park.

JUSTIN Well, text her. It'll be here any minute.

LIAM No, don't bother. Here she comes. Hurry up, Nicole!

NICOLE Sorry I'm late. You'll never guess what just happened to me.

EMMA What?

NICOLE I'll tell you on the bus after I catch my breath. Oh, I'm so excited!!

EMMA OK, tell us what happened.

NICOLE Guess.

LIAM Guess?

NICOLE Yes, we've got some time to kill. Come on, bet you can't guess.

JUSTIN You were abducted by aliens, but they took one look at you and brought you right back.

NICOLE Ha, ha. Very funny. But surprisingly enough, you're wrong.

EMMA OK, you were halfway here when you realized you'd forgotten your phone, so you had to go back and get it.

NICOLE No, but that's a pretty good guess. Try again.

LIAM I know. You stopped at the supermarket to buy us chips or candy or something. Please say I'm right. I'm starving!

NICOLE No, sorry.

EMMA This is way too difficult. I hate guessing.

JUSTIN Got it! You ran into Ben Anderson and stopped to talk to him.

LIAM Who on earth is Ben Anderson?

JUSTIN That new guy in Mrs. Brooks' class. Tall, dark hair, athletic. Nicole really likes him.

LIAM Oh really? Tell us more!

NICOLE It's none of your business, Liam. And in any case, Justin's wrong. Well, about why I'm late, at least. More guesses!

EMMA No, Nicole, we give up. You're going to tell us eventually anyway.

NICOLE Fair enough. You ready? I am going to be on television tonight! On the news!

LIAM You're what?

JUSTIN Yeah, right.

NICOLE No, really. I'm going to be on the news!

DEVELOPING SPEAKING

3 Work in pairs. Discuss what happens next in the story. Write down your ideas.

We think they watch the news, but Nicole isn't on.

4 ◼◀ EP4 Watch to find out what happens.

5 Answer the questions.

1 Why does Emma ask Justin, "Don't you ever watch the news?"
2 What time do they meet at Nicole's house?
3 What does Nicole tell the reporter?
4 Who sends Emma a text and a video?
5 Why is Nicole embarrassed by the video?

PHRASES FOR FLUENCY

1 Find these expressions in the photostory. Who says them? How do you say them in your language?

1 don't bother _____
2 … or something _____
3 … on earth … _____
4 It's none of (your) business. _____
5 … in any case, … _____
6 …, at least _____

2 Use the expressions in Exercise 1 to complete the sentences.

1 Why _____ did you dye your hair green?
2 Can you lend me $20? Or $5, _____ ?
3 There's no Wi-Fi in the camp where we're going, so _____ writing me any emails.
4 I'm bored. Let's go swimming _____ .
5 I don't really want to go to the party, and _____ I haven't been invited.
6 Stop asking me questions! _____ !

WordWise

Expressions with *way*

1 Look at these sentences from the unit so far. Complete them with the phrases from the list.

the way | the same way | in my way
on my way | either way | way too

1 Twitter allows people who think _____ to get together.
2 Liam, you're _____ . I can't see the screen.
3 I was _____ to meet you when I saw him.
4 This is _____ difficult. I hate guessing.

5 How is Twitter changing _____ we do things?
6 It doesn't really matter _____ .

2 Which phrase in Exercise 1 means:

1 in a similar manner
2 very / really
3 coming
4 between me and something else
5 the manner or method
6 in any version of the situation

3 Choose the correct options.

1 Please move! You're *in a way / in my way*.
2 He dances *the same way / in a way* he sings – badly!
3 He called me and told me that he's *in his way / on his way* here. He'll be ten minutes.
4 I really like *the way / in your way* you've done your hair!
5 I don't really care. *Either way / The way* works for me.
6 Can you turn the TV down please? It's *the way / way too* loud!

Workbook page 92 ➡

FUNCTIONS

Introducing news

1 Complete these sentences from the photostory and video. Use the same word in both sentences.

1 **Nicole** You'll never _____ what happened.
2 **Emma** Yes, and _____ what? She videoed it.

2 Complete the sentences with the words in the list. Use each word only once.

know | heard | about | guess | believe

1 Have you _____ ?
2 Have you heard _____ Jim's brother?
3 Did you _____ that they're going to close the movie theater?
4 _____ !
5 You'll never _____ what I found out.

3 SPEAKING Work in pairs. Think of three surprising pieces of news (real or pretend).

A tells a piece of news to B with an introduction. B replies. Then switch roles.

LISTENING

Part 4: Multiple choice

Workbook page 89 ▶

1 🔊 2.25 **You will hear an interview with a teenager named Luiza Vargas about the "Good News Project."** **For questions 1–7, choose the best answer (A, B, or C).**

1 What is the Good News Project?
   A a newspaper that only reports stories to make people happy
   B a plan to find and share positive news stories
   C an attempt to get happy stories onto the television news

2 What contributed most to Luiza starting the project?
   A She was fed up with hearing only good news.
   B She wanted to stop people complaining about the news.
   C She wanted to change the way her school magazine reported stories.

3 What did the local newspaper initially agree to?
   A giving her idea a try to see if it would be popular with their readers
   B getting her involved with the local radio station
   C publishing five stories each week

4 What is Luiza's involvement with the radio station?
   A She reads the local news every morning.
   B She prepares one story every day for them.
   C She writes their news stories.

5 What does Luiza find most difficult about the project?
   A coordinating her team of reporters
   B deciding which stories to give to the newspaper and radio station
   C checking that the stories are reliable

6 What should someone do if they have a story for the project?
   A write it up and send it in
   B be sure that it is accurate
   C give it to one of the students at Luiza's school

7 Which of these stories would the Good News Project NOT report?
   A Number of people attending church decreases
   B Zoo welcomes new baby elephant
   C Schoolchildren find home for homeless man

WRITING

Part 2: A review

2 **You have seen this ad on a website for teenagers.**

   Write your review (140–190 words).

Contest

Tell us about a movie you have seen recently. Tell us briefly what it's about and who's in it. Would you recommend it? Why or why not?

The best review will be put online next month.

Movie Review

Workbook page 97 ▶

TEST YOURSELF

VOCABULARY

1 Complete the sentences with the words in the list. There are four extra words.

regretted | pass | major | blame | front | let | wanted
way | apologize | living | live | give | denied | career

1 Sam wants to be a science teacher, so he is planning to _____ in chemistry.
2 Rosanna is very ambitious. She won't let anything get in the _____ of her career.
3 As soon as you have any news, please _____ me a call.
4 Ms. Eberly's car broke down, so she had to _____ to the class for being late.
5 The movie was terrible. I really _____ going to see it.
6 My _____ counselor did a good job of helping me choose my courses.
7 I don't know when we'll be arriving, but I'll _____ you know as soon as I can.
8 Mick told the policeman he didn't know the bank robber. He _____ having met him at all.
9 The hotel looked great on the website. But unfortunately, it didn't _____ up to our expectations.
10 If you leave cookies on a low table, you can't _____ the dog for eating them.

/10

GRAMMAR

2 Complete the sentences with the words in the list. There are two extra words.

hadn't | will | didn't | was | wouldn't | would | wasn't | had

1 I feel sick. If only I _____ eaten so much!
2 David said he _____ seen Michael the day before. They ate lunch together.
3 Liz asked Victor if he _____ be at the soccer game that afternoon.
4 I'm sure I'd understand if only my French teacher _____ speak so fast.
5 The security guard asked Sol why he _____ standing around outside the bank.
6 Mr. Jones called the office to say that, unfortunately, he _____ be able to attend the meeting.

3 Find and correct the mistake in each sentence.

1 I'd rather had a quick salad and then go back to work.
2 I wish he doesn't give me so many presents – it was so embarrassing.
3 Sheila said the movie on TV the day before was excellent.
4 They announced that the president will make a speech before tomorrow's ceremony.
5 I'd rather you come by my house, if that's possible.
6 He accused me to break his camera.

/12

FUNCTIONAL LANGUAGE

4 Choose the correct options.

1 A You'll never *know / guess* what happened to me yesterday.
  B What? Did they ask you *to play / playing* baseball for the Yankees?
2 A I'd *rather / prefer* you played that music more quietly.
  B Well, I'd *rather / prefer* it if you went to your own room.
3 A I'd rather you *didn't / don't* stay in bed any longer.
  B But I don't want to get up! I'd prefer *to go / I went* back to sleep.
4 A Have you *heard / seen* the article in the paper about Jack's accident?
  B Yes, I have, but do you *hear / know* how it really happened?

/8

MY SCORE **/30**

| 22 – 30 |
| 10 – 21 |
| 0 – 9 |

11 SPACE AND BEYOND

OBJECTIVES

FUNCTIONS: sympathizing about past situations

GRAMMAR: speculating (past, present, and future); cause and effect linkers

VOCABULARY: space idioms; adjectives commonly used to describe movies

READING

1 SPEAKING **Look at the photo and discuss in pairs.**

1 Can you describe what's happening in the picture?

2 How would you feel if you were the astronaut?

3 If you were offered the chance to go into space, would you take it? Why or why not?

2 SPEAKING **Discuss in small groups.**

1 If there is life on other planets, what do you think it is like?

2 Would it be a good idea to make contact with extraterrestrial life forms? Explain your reasons.

3 Read the article quickly. Are any of your opinions mentioned in the article?

4 2.26 **Read the article again and listen. Mark the statements T (true) or F (false). Then work with a partner and correct the false statements.**

1 Whether there is life on other planets is a question that divides people. ☐

2 Stephen Hawking is completely sure that we are not alone in the universe. ☐

3 Hawking believes that the majority of life forms on other planets will be very basic. ☐

4 He says that any alien visitors to Earth would clearly have more advanced technology than we do. ☐

5 He believes alien visitors might try and make Earth their new home. ☐

6 He uses an example from history to illustrate his point. ☐

5 SPEAKING **Work in pairs and answer the questions.**

1 What do you think would most impress aliens visiting our planet?

2 What would least impress them?

They might not come in peace . . .

Whether there is life on other planets is one of the great mysteries of our time. Some people are sure that other life forms exist and say they may have already visited us. There are people who believe that aliens must have built things like the pyramids because of the technology involved. A significant number of people claim to have seen strange spaceships in the sky, and some even claim that they have been abducted by aliens. Of course, there are also many people who believe that other life forms can't exist and that Earth is the only inhabited planet in the whole universe.

One man who thinks that other forms of life are almost certain to be "out there" is one of the world's most famous scientists, Stephen Hawking. And he thinks we should be worried, very worried. He believes that aliens are very likely to exist – but instead of trying to find them, we should be doing everything we can to hide from them. He thinks they might not be quite as friendly as we like to imagine.

The universe, Hawking explains, has 100 billion galaxies. Each one of them contains hundreds of millions of stars. In such a big place, Earth can't be the only planet with life on it. Most life forms, he thinks, will be simple, single-celled organisms – the sort of life that has lived on Earth for most of its history. But with so many different life forms out there, some could be intelligent, and some could even be dangerous. And if they are out there, Hawking believes that contact with them might be the end for us.

If aliens have the technology to travel the extensive distances required to reach us, then, in his opinion, they are bound to have the technology to build better weapons than us. They might only see Earth as a place with valuable resources. They may simply come to Earth, take what they want, destroy the rest, and then leave again. He argues, "We only have to look at ourselves to see how intelligent life might develop into something we wouldn't want to meet."

Hawking warns that trying to make contact with other life forms might be "a little too risky." He said, "If aliens ever visit us, I think the result will be like when Christopher Columbus first landed in America, and that didn't turn out very well for the Native Americans."

Hawking is not the only one who believes there is intelligent life in outer space. Lord Rees, another famous scientist, recently asserted that aliens could be so advanced that they might exist in forms that are too complicated for us to understand. So maybe it's time to forget our ideas of little green men who "come in peace," turn off the radio signals we're sending into space, forget about sending rockets outside of our solar system, and hope that we really are alone in the universe.

■ TRAIN TO THINK ■

Spotting flawed arguments

There are many different ways that people can try to convince you that something is true without using actual evidence. Here are three common ways:

A **The ignorance argument:** Not being able to disprove something doesn't mean it's true. It may be true, but you can't say for certain unless there is evidence.

B **Judging by emotions:** Just because someone has strong emotions or deeply held beliefs doesn't mean that what they say is true. Think carefully about their argument, and don't let their emotions persuade you.

C **Quoting an authority:** Sometimes experts or their work is quoted and used as evidence that something is true. But these people can make mistakes, too. Or their work could be taken out of context. Be careful – "experts" are often used in advertising to try to sell things to you!

1 **Read the quotations and match them with explanations A–C above.**

1 "I saw this scientist on TV. He says that we should eat more fatty foods." ☐

2 "I really dislike politicians and never believe anything they say." ☐

3 A "I didn't take your phone."
  B "You must have taken it. I didn't see anyone else in the room." ☐

2 **SPEAKING** **Work in pairs. For each of the statements below, create three different flawed arguments (A, B, and C) to support it.**

1 Spiders make good pets.
2 Tall people are healthier.
3 Money always brings unhappiness.

> *The man in the pet store says I should buy a tarantula from him because they are really easy to take care of.*

> *Spiders really are the most fascinating creatures on the planet. I love them.*

> *I can't think of any reason why we shouldn't get one.*

GRAMMAR
Speculating (past, present, and future)

1 **Complete the sentences with the words in the list. Then complete the rule.**

must have | bound to | certain to | very likely
might be | can't be | may have already

1 They _____ visited us.
2 Aliens _____ built things like the pyramids.
3 He believes that aliens are _____ to exist.
4 Earth _____ the only planet with life on it.
5 Other forms of life are almost _____ be "out there."
6 Contact with them _____ the end for us.
7 They are _____ have the technology to build better weapons than us.

> **RULE:** To speculate we often use the modal verbs *might, may, could, must,* and *can't.*
> - *might, may,* and ¹_____ refer to possibility
> - ²_____ refers to a perceived impossibility
> - ³_____ refers to a perceived certainty
>
> When we refer to past events, the modals are followed by ⁴_____ + past participle.
>
> When we refer to present or future events, the modals are followed by ⁵_____.
>
> We can also use *be + bound to / *⁶_____ *to / likely to* to speculate about past, present, and future events.

2 **Match the sentence pairs.**

1 They must have gotten lost.
2 They can't have gotten lost.
3 Jim's certain to know a good restaurant.
4 Jim's bound to be late.
5 The forecast says it's likely to rain.
6 You must be hungry.
7 You can't be hungry.

a He eats out all the time.
b He always is.
c So take an umbrella.
d You haven't eaten all day.
e They're more than two hours late.
f We just had lunch.
g They've made this trip hundreds of times.

Pronunciation
Sentence stress: modals for speculation
Go to page 121.

3 **SPEAKING** How possible do you think these things are? Discuss with a partner and put them in order of probability.

- humans landing on Mars in the next ten years
- a world free of pollution
- you going abroad on vacation this year

> *I don't think humans are likely to land on Mars in the next ten years.*

> *Why not? We might invent new spaceships.*

Workbook page 100

FUNCTIONS
Sympathizing about past situations

1 **Match the sentences and the replies.**

1 Andy didn't pass his driving test. ☐
2 So when I went to check in, I realized I'd left my passport at home. ☐
3 The movie had already started by the time they got there. ☐

a *What a shame.* They must have been disappointed.
b *Poor thing.* He must have been upset.
c *How awful.* You must have been so annoyed.

2 **Put the conversation in order.**

☐ AMY I wasn't. I didn't even have a book with me.
[1] AMY You won't believe what happened to me on my way home.
☐ AMY I didn't get home until midnight. My mom was waiting up for me.
☐ AMY It was. And to make things worse, my phone was dead.
☐ AMY She was. And of course, I couldn't call to let her know what was happening.
☐ AMY I missed my train and had to wait three hours for the next one.
☐ TOM *Oh no.* You had to wait for three hours? How awful. That *must have* been boring.
☐ TOM What? You poor thing. You *can't have* been happy about that.
☐ TOM Oh dear. She *must have* been worried.
☐ TOM What happened?
☐ TOM So you must have gotten home really late.

3 **Think of an annoying thing that happened to you recently. Make notes about what happened.**

4 **SPEAKING** Work in pairs. Tell each other your stories and sympathize.

LISTENING

1 SPEAKING Discuss in pairs. What would aliens learn about humans based on these pictures?

2 ◁)) 2.29 You're going to hear someone talking about the Voyager mission. What was special about the Voyager mission? What did the spaceship take with it?

3 ◁)) 2.29 Listen again and complete the sentences.

1 Voyager I and II were originally sent into space to explore _____ and _____.

2 Each of the Voyager spaceships contained _____.

3 The idea was that aliens could learn about the _____ from the information.

4 The discs contained _____ in 55 different languages.

5 As an example of animal life on Earth, sound recordings of wild _____ were sent.

6 Most of the music that was chosen was _____.

7 Aliens will know how to use the discs because they contain _____.

8 We probably won't know what any aliens think of all this for at least _____ years.

■ THiNK SELF-ESTEEM ■
Who we are

1 SPEAKING Work in pairs. You are on a committee to decide what to put on a new disc to be sent up on the next Voyager. Decide on the following things:

- three pieces of music
- three sound clips
- three books
- five images
- one special item

2 SPEAKING Compare your ideas with another pair and decide on a final list. Justify your choices.

VOCABULARY
Space idioms

1 Match the sentence pairs.

1 Jen's been accepted into Cambridge University. ☐

2 You can count on Mike. ☐

3 The special effects in the new *Star Wars* movie are amazing. ☐

4 Anyone can boil an egg. ☐

5 We very rarely go to the movies. ☐

6 He thinks every girl he meets is "Miss Right." ☐

a They're *out of this world.*

b *It isn't rocket science.*

c *Once in a blue moon,* I'd say.

d He's very *starry-eyed.*

e She's *on cloud nine.*

f He's very *down to earth* and reliable.

2 Match the expressions in italics in Exercise 1 with the definitions.

☐ 1 hardly ever

☐ 2 not complicated or difficult

☐ 3 really happy

☐ 4 incredible

☐ 5 overly romantic / overly optimistic

☐ 6 normal (not at all pretentious)

Workbook page 102 →

READING

1 Read the blog. Which film does the writer consider the greatest space movie of all time?

My all-time favorite movies about space

It isn't every day you get a full lunar eclipse. So to get you in the mood for tomorrow's astronomical event, I'm suggesting a few of my all-time favorite movies about space. Believe me, they don't get any better than this.

Apollo 13 (1995)

When Tom Hanks announces, "Houston, we have a problem," you know you're in for a *thrilling* ride. This movie is based on the true story of the Apollo 13 mission to the moon, which very nearly ended in disaster. One of the rocket's oxygen tanks explodes, and consequently, the three-man crew has to fight against all odds to bring their spaceship home. Of course, we know they make it, but that doesn't make it any less exciting to watch. It gets a little *sentimental* at the end, but after what they've been through, they deserve a few tears of joy.

WALL-E (2008)

Only Pixar could produce a movie about environmental destruction that manages to be light-hearted and fun. When the movie starts, the Earth is a mess as a result of mankind's greed, and the last humans have escaped in a giant spaceship into outer space. They've left behind an army of robots to clean away the garbage in the hope that one day humans can return. WALL-E is one of these robots, but his daily routine is interrupted by the arrival of EVE, a robot sent to see what progress has been made. WALL-E falls in love, but will EVE return his love, and between them, can they offer hope for the human race? Of course, this *delightful* and entertaining animated film is aimed at kids, but it can be equally enjoyed by adults.

Avatar (2009)

When it comes to *action-packed* blockbusters, James Cameron's movies are masterpieces, and the sci-fi thriller *Avatar* is no exception. Forget little green aliens, Cameron's aliens are blue and super cool. Mankind has invaded the planet Pandora because of its natural resources, and Pandora's native inhabitants are fighting back. It gets a little *far-fetched* at times, but Cameron's Pandora is *breathtaking,* and the eco-message is a reminder to all of us of how important it is that we take care of our own planet.

The Martian (2015)

I've saved the best for last. Matt Damon plays astronaut Mark Watney, who is part of a space mission to explore Mars. Due to an accident during a big storm, he gets injured and separated from the rest of the crew. Deciding that he must be dead, they return home without him. Watney must now somehow survive everything the planet can throw at him and try and find a way of making contact with his base back on Earth. Two things set this film apart from the rest: its *stunning* special effects and Damon's *memorable* performance. Although it's best seen on the big screen in 3-D, even on the small screen this is easily the best space movie of all time.

2 Read the blog again. Which movie …

1 is a love story?
2 involves a fight between two races?
3 does the writer suggest might make you cry?
4 involves a character left on his own?
5 does the writer suggest contains an important lesson for us?
6 does the writer suggest is for all ages?
7 does the writer suggest is best seen at a movie theater?
8 is about something that actually happened?

3 SPEAKING Work in pairs. Discuss the questions.

1 Which of these movies have you seen or would you like to see?
2 Which movies do you think are missing from the list?
3 Why does the writer refer to these movies as space movies rather than sci-fi movies?
4 What do you think is the best sci-fi movie of all time?

GRAMMAR
Cause and effect linkers

1 **Complete the sentences with the missing word or phrase. Then look back at the blog to check your answers and complete the rule.**

1 _____ an accident during a big storm, he gets injured and separated from the rest of the crew.
2 The Earth is a mess _____ mankind's greed.
3 Mankind has invaded the planet Pandora _____ its natural resources.
4 One of the rocket's oxygen tanks explodes, and _____ the three-man crew have to fight against all odds to bring their spaceship home.

> **RULE:** We use linkers such as *due to*, *as a result of*, *because of*, and *consequently* to link actions and their consequences.
>
> *Due to*, *as a result of*, and [1]_____ can come at the beginning of a sentence or in the middle between the two clauses. They are followed by the reason for an action or event.
>
> These linkers are usually followed by a noun phrase. *Due to* and *as a result of* are more formal than *because of*.
>
> [2]_____ generally comes at the beginning of a new sentence or clause. It introduces the effect of the cause mentioned in the previous sentence. It is followed by a clause (subject and verb).

2 ✱ **Complete the second sentence so that it has a similar meaning to the first sentence using the word in parentheses. You must use between two and five words including the word given.**

0 Paul ate too much. He felt sick. (result)
As a *result of eating* too much, Paul felt sick.
1 Olivia didn't get into the college she wanted. Her bad grades were the main reason. (because)
_____, Olivia didn't get into the college she wanted.
2 The weather was bad, so the race was canceled. (due)
The race was canceled _____ .
3 Jack had a bad cold. He didn't go to school. (of)
Jack didn't go to school _____ cold.
4 The police got some information and arrested the man. (result)
The man was arrested _____ information given to the police.
5 Too many people were on vacation, so the meeting was postponed. (due)
The meeting was postponed _____ so many people being on vacation.

Workbook page 101

VOCABULARY
Adjectives commonly used to describe movies

1 **Match the words in italics from the blog with the definitions below.**

1 really pleasant _____
2 really beautiful _____
3 really exciting _____
4 over-emotional _____
5 difficult to believe _____
6 really exciting and really beautiful _____
7 something you won't forget _____
8 full of action _____

2 **Choose the correct word to complete each sentence.**

1 The ending of the movie was really *thrilling* / *sentimental*. I was on the edge of my seat.
2 I was surprised that the ending was so *stunning* / *sentimental*. It was a horror movie, after all.
3 It's a *delightful* / *far-fetched* film. I loved every minute of it.
4 It's full of explosions and fights and car chases. It's a really *action-packed* / *delightful* movie.
5 I know it was a fantasy film, but for me the story was so *far-fetched* / *memorable* that it just seemed ridiculous.
6 The characters were kind of dull, but the costumes were *thrilling* / *stunning*.
7 It's a really *sentimental* / *memorable* movie. I'm sure I'll be thinking about it for days.
8 The opening scenes are *action-packed* / *breathtaking*. They're absolutely beautiful.

3 **Work in pairs. Think of a movie as an example for each of the sentences in Exercise 2.**

Workbook page 102

SPEAKING

Work in pairs. Choose one of the categories and think of four movies for it. As you discuss your choices, use the adjectives in Exercise 2 to help you describe the movies and agree on your final list.

The four greatest comedies
The four greatest romantic movies
The four greatest action movies
The four greatest horror movies

Culture

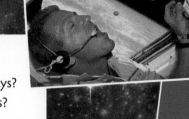

1 **Scan the article to find the answers to these questions.**

1 What countries are engaged in space exploration these days?

2 What are some of the everyday problems in space stations?

2 🔊 2.30 **Read and listen to check.**

Real Humans

Life ... in space

For decades space travel was a race between the United States and the former Soviet Union. But these days other nations such as China, Japan, and India have joined in the ᵃquest to learn more about the universe beyond Earth. And then, of course, there are private businesses selling space trips for huge ᵇprofits to the few people who can afford them and the very few who are eager to ᶜembark on such an extreme adventure.

In the media astronauts are ᵈportrayed as heroes. That's why in today's *Real Humans* column, we go behind the scenes and beyond the glory to find out what life in a space station is really like.

The sushi disaster

Food in space can be rather boring. That's why astronauts are allowed a ᵉbonus container with a few of their favorite dishes. In 2007 astronaut Sunita Williams took along some sushi and a tube of wasabi paste, the famous spicy green paste that is commonly eaten with sushi. Because there's no gravity, when she ᶠsqueezed the tube, the paste came out and went everywhere. She managed to clean most of it off the walls, but the smell remained for quite a while. Consequently, wasabi was put on a list of forbidden space foods because it is considered "too dangerous."

The shower that isn't

Hygiene can be a challenge in space. There are no showers, of course, because water won't run down your body like it does in your bathroom. Without gravity, the solution lies in water guns similar to the ones children sometimes play with. With the help of this "toy" and a washcloth, astronauts can shoot water at themselves and get clean.

ᵍDrifting off

Even astronauts have to sleep. Although sleeping in a gravity-free environment can be quite comfortable, it also poses problems. As Canadian astronaut Julie Payette once told reporters, "We sleep very well in space. Can you imagine? We have a sleeping bag each, and when you get into it, you float in the sleeping bag. The sleeping bag floats in the module. So all you have to do is just attach it somewhere, which is a good idea, by the way, because during the night while you're sleeping, you might start drifting and end up somewhere you didn't intend to be."

Roller coaster space rides

Free-floating in the space station can be quite enjoyable, but the trips to and from the station can be a little rough. The Russian Soyuz spacecraft has a particular ʰreputation for offering rather bumpy rides. NASA astronaut Tracy Caldwell Dyson said, "I've heard it described as a train wreck followed by a car crash followed by falling off your bike." After she flew home from the station on one herself, she reported, "It certainly didn't disappoint!"

3 **Answer the questions.**

1 Who do private businesses sell trips into space to?

2 What was the problem with the wasabi that an astronaut tried to eat?

3 Why can't astronauts have normal showers?

4 What advantages are there to sleeping in a space station?

5 How do astronauts sleep in the space station?

6 What did astronaut Tracy Caldwell Dyson mean when she said, "It certainly didn't disappoint!"?

4 VOCABULARY **Match the highlighted words in the article to the definitions.**

- [ ] 1 to set off on a journey
- [ ] 2 the money a business earns minus costs
- [ ] 3 the way that people or things are generally perceived
- [ ] 4 pressed something hard
- [ ] 5 floating or falling asleep
- [ ] 6 mission / expedition to find something
- [ ] 7 something extra you get at no cost
- [ ] 8 the way someone or something is shown to be

SPEAKING

Work in pairs. Discuss the questions.

1 Which of the four examples of life in a space station would be the biggest challenge for you? Why?

2 Would you like to spend time in a space station if it was possible? Why or why not?

3 Can you think of any other aspects of daily life that would be difficult in space?

WRITING
A report

1 Read the report. What problem does it present and what solution does it suggest?

> **[1]** The aim of this report is to discuss a problem recently encountered during the Admiral 9 mission to the International Space Station and make suggestions about what can be done to prevent this from happening in the future.
>
> **[2]** In September of this year, commander Captain Janice Logan reported a serious incident of computer malfunction in the dining quarters of the International Space Station. On further inspection it appeared that the computer had stopped working due to it being covered in a thick orange liquid. Logan questioned members of her team only to discover that the problem had occurred when engineer Ian Coyne's carrot soup had leaked from its container and found its way to the computing area.
>
> **[3]** Although the crew was able to run the back-up computer, the incident has raised serious concerns about dining habits. Consequently, while a more detailed report is being prepared, we suggest an immediate ban on all liquid food aboard the space station until safer procedures can be introduced.

2 Match the paragraphs with their main function. There are two extra functions.

- [ ] Say who is responsible
- [ ] A brief description of what the report is about
- [ ] Suggestions for changes
- [ ] Talk about the cost of making changes
- [ ] An outline of the problem

3 Use the words in parentheses to rewrite the sentences in your notebook. Make sure they have the same meaning.

The computer had stopped working <u>due to it</u> being covered in a thick orange liquid.

1 (as a result of)
2 (because of)

<u>Although</u> the crew was able to run the back-up computer, the incident has raised serious concerns about dining habits.

3 (however)
4 (despite)

4 Read through the situation and make notes.

Last Friday there was a school trip to the space museum. The bus was supposed to leave at 9 a.m. but didn't leave until 10 a.m. because five students were late. As a consequence, the group had an hour less to spend at the museum.

Problem: _____

Solution: _____

5 Write a report (140–190 words) about the problem with the school trip. Don't forget to:

- say what the report is about
- outline the problem
- suggest a solution

READING

1 Look at the photos. What do they show? In which parts of the world can they be found? Have you ever seen any of them in real life?

2 Read the article quickly. Check your answers to Exercise 1.

3 ◀》2.31 Read the article again and listen. Answer the questions.

1 Why has the Voronya Cave not been completely explored?

2 Why is more known about the caves in Europe, the U.S., and Australia than those in other parts of the world?

3 For what two reasons is the deep ocean difficult for people to explore?

4 How much of the ocean floor remains unexplored?

5 Why is the Amazon rainforest of such great interest to biologists?

6 What can exploration of Greenland help with?

7 What are the "tragic outcomes" of some desert expeditions?

8 What's special about the animals and plants that exist in deserts?

4 SPEAKING Work in pairs. Discuss the questions.

1 Why do you think the places in the article are more accessible now than they were before?

2 Can you think of any other relatively undiscovered places on Earth?

3 Which of the places in the article would you most / least like to visit? Why?

Our undiscovered world

Over the centuries we have discovered more and more about our world, and it's easy to think that everything that could be discovered already has been. But that's not true. The world holds many more secrets – secrets that are waiting to be revealed. Here we discuss five places that have yet to be opened up completely.

Caves

Deep, dark, cold, and often uninhabitable, caves remain one of the least explored and least documented places on Earth. The deepest known cave in the world is Voronya Cave in the central Asian country of Georgia, which is so inaccessible and inhospitable that very little is known about it.

The exact number of caves on Earth is yet to be determined. Caving is a very popular activity in Europe, Australia, and the United States, so most of the caves currently documented are from those parts of the world. However, thousands of caves are thought to exist in China. Most of these remain unexplored.

The Mariana Trench

The deepest and darkest place in the ocean is the 11,000-meter-deep Mariana Trench. Due to freezing temperatures and immense water pressure, the deep ocean is totally hostile to humans. Although technological advances have led to the discovery of many new varieties of deep-sea creatures on the ocean floor, there is a lot more to be learned. In fact, only two percent of the ocean floor has been explored. More is known about our solar system than about our oceans. But of course, as further studies are conducted, we will understand more about life in harsh ocean conditions.

The Amazon rainforest

The Amazon rainforest is said to comprise about 50 percent of all the rainforests in the world. Its vast biodiversity supports a huge number of species of plants, and more than 2,000 species of birds and mammals are known to live there. Interest in its climate and resources has resulted in many large exploratory expeditions. However, due to its inaccessibility, full exploration of the region has been almost impossible. Up to now, about 2.5 million insect species and 400,000 plant species have been officially documented, but tens of thousands more are believed to live there, waiting to be found.

Greenland

About 81 percent of Greenland is covered in ice, so it is almost completely unpopulated, and the relatively small number of people who do live there tend to live only on the ice-free coast. Greenland has only been explored to a limited extent, as the climate is quite unsuitable for human life. Although research expeditions are currently being carried out in the northern parts of the country, the most interesting research in Greenland might tell us more about the past than the present. Tubes of ice have been drilled out of the deepest ancient ice, giving scientists a record of the Earth's environment that goes back thousands of years.

Deserts

Although we know where all the Earth's deserts are, they are among the most unwelcoming environments for human beings, so very few explorations have been conducted. It is virtually impossible to survive long periods of time in the desert, and consequently, desert explorations have frequently had tragic outcomes – many people are known to have died on such expeditions. It's unclear whether anything of particular interest would be uncovered by further investigations into deserts, although there are animal and plant species there that are distinctive because they have developed to survive in very high temperatures and with very little water.

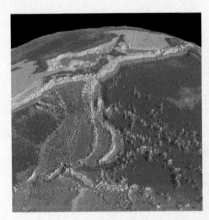  

■ TRAIN TO THINK ■

Exploring hidden messages

People don't always say what they mean. For example, imagine you show a short story you've written to a friend and ask for their opinion. What do you think when they tell you, "I thought the beginning was great"? Was the beginning really good, or are they trying to hide the fact that they didn't really like the rest of it? People do this for a number of reasons; they don't want to be rude, they're not brave enough to tell the truth, or they don't really have an opinion.

1 **Look at what these people have said. What do you think they might really think?**

1 *That's an interesting sweater you're wearing.*
2 *There's an earlier train you could catch, if you want.*
3 *Joe always has a lot to say for himself.*
4 *Your homework reminded me a lot of Simon's.*

2 **Read the situations. What could you say without being too direct?**

1 You're at your friend's house for dinner. His mom cooks you something you really don't like.
2 Your best friend asks you what you think about his new haircut. You think it's awful.
3 Your dad is wearing a really ugly sweater.
4 Your aunt's annoying dog keeps barking.

GRAMMAR
Passive report structures

1   **Find and underline the sentences in the article that mean the same as 1–5. Then complete the rule with *written*, *past*, or *present*.**

1   People believe that tens of thousands more live there.
2   People think that thousands of caves exist in China.
3   Experts say that the Amazon rainforest comprises about 50 percent of all the rainforests in the world.
4   We know that over 2,000 species of birds and mammals live there.
5   We know that many people died on such expeditions.

RULE: An example of a passive report structure is:

*Thousands of caves **are thought to exist** in China.*

We can also say:

***It is thought** that thousands of caves exist in China.*

These structures use reporting verbs like *say*, *think*, *believe*, *know*, and *consider*.

If we use a passive report structure to talk about beliefs or knowledge of ¹_____ actions, we use the correct form of *be* + past participle of the reporting verb + infinitive:

*She **is said to be** one of the greatest climbers of all time.*

***It is said** that she is one of the greatest climbers of all time.*

If we use a passive report structure to talk about beliefs or knowledge of ²_____ actions, we use the correct form of *be* + past participle of the reporting verb + *to* + *have* + past participle:

*Many people **are known to have died** on the expedition.*

Passive report structures are more often used in ³_____ language, such as newspaper reports.

2   **Rewrite the sentences using passive report structures.**

0   Experts know that Death Valley is the hottest place on the planet.
    Death Valley *is known to be the hottest place on the planet* .

1   We believe that the ice in Antarctica is disappearing.
    The ice in Antarctica _____ .

2   People say that this cave is 500 meters deep.
    This cave _____ .

3   Experts think that most fish in the deep ocean are blind.
    Most fish _____ .

4   We know that the Sahara Desert contained water only 5,000 years ago.
    The Sahara Desert _____ .

5   Experts believe that some deep-sea creatures have existed for millions of years.
    Some deep-sea creatures _____ .

Workbook page 108

VOCABULARY
Geographical features

1   **Match the words with the photos. Write 1–8 in the boxes.**

1 reef | 2 bay | 3 sand dune | 4 canyon
5 waterfall | 6 mountain range
7 volcano | 8 glacier

2   **Complete each sentence with a word from Exercise 1.**

1   There's often snow on the top of a very high _____ .

2   It can be difficult to run up a _____ because it isn't solid ground.

3   When water goes over a _____ , it often looks white.

4   A _____ can be dangerous for ships because it's close to the surface of the ocean.

5   If a _____ is active, it sometimes erupts and can be very dangerous.

6   It can take a very long time for a _____ to move even as little as ten centimeters.

7   A _____ is a good place for ships to stop, because it's protected by land on three sides.

8   There's usually a river at the bottom of a _____ .

3   **SPEAKING   Work in pairs. You have three minutes to think of as many famous examples of these features as you can. Then compare your ideas with other pairs.**

Workbook page 110

LISTENING
Discovering new species

1 **Match the photos and the names.**

Queen Alexandra's butterfly | honeyeater
monitor lizard | rainbow fish | tree frog | river shark

2 **Which of the creatures do you think are:**

beautiful? poisonous? endangered? dangerous?

3 🔊 2.32 **Listen to someone giving a talk about discovering new species in Papua New Guinea. Which three creatures in the photos are mentioned?**

4 🔊 2.32 **Listen again and answer the questions.**

1 Who does the speaker work for?
2 How many new species were found in Papua New Guinea between 1998 and 2008?
3 Why wasn't the honeyeater found earlier?
4 What does the speaker say is the "good news"?
5 She says, "It's human beings who are doing it." Doing what?

FUNCTIONS
Speaking persuasively

1 🔊 2.33 **Listen again to the end of the talk. Complete the text.**

"… and so these animals find it harder and harder to live. The ¹_____ of this will be more and more animals becoming extinct – and that's a ²_____ thought. If we ³_____ now, to stop habitats from being destroyed, many animals will disappear, and future generations will only see them in books. I think it's ⁴_____ for humans to find ways to live well but without harming other living creatures, ⁵_____?"

2 **In the extract from the talk in Exercise 1, find:**

1 adjectives and adverbs used to make a point more strongly
2 a question tag
3 a conditional clause to show urgency

3 **Write two or three sentences from a speech where someone wants to persuade listeners that:**

1 traffic has to be reduced in a town
2 having a new supermarket in a town is a bad idea
3 a sports stadium is needed in a town

Pronunciation

Flapping *t* and *d*
Go to page 121. 🔊

◼ THiNK VALUES ◼
Human activity and the natural world

1 **Read what the speaker says toward the end of her talk. Then think about the questions. Make notes.**

"Forests are being turned into fields to grow food, trees are being cut down for the wood, and rivers are being used by more and more boats, and so these animals find it harder and harder to live."

1 Can you think of any examples of what she's describing?
2 What other problems can human activity cause (not just problems for animals)?
3 What problems might people encounter when they explore the deep ocean? Or caves?

SPEAKING

Work in pairs or small groups.

1 Use your notes from Exercise 1. Decide which question you are most interested in.
2 Together, prepare a two-minute presentation entitled "Human activity and the natural world."
3 Give your presentation to the class.

READING

1 **SPEAKING** Work in pairs. Discuss what you know about when the main roads, railways, and telephone lines were built in your country. Think about …

   1 how and when the main roads (and/or railways) were built, and by whom.

   2 how communications, such as telephone lines, started, and when.

   3 any difficulties people had when building the roads, telephone lines, etc.

2 Look at the title and pictures. What do you think Rondon achieved?

DISCOVERERS

A friend to native people
Cândido Rondon

Almost every country on our planet has been explored and mapped, and all of these have roads, railways, and lines of communication. It can be hard for us to imagine the people who explored places without all of the infrastructure that we now take for granted.

This series celebrates the men and women who opened the world up and risked their lives to protect the people and environments they discovered along the way. This week, we profile a man not well known outside his own country and continent – Cândido Rondon.

In 1865, in a small village in the state of Mato Grosso, Brazil, a boy was born. His father was of Portuguese ancestry, and his mother was a native Brazilian. Who could have known that his origins would play such a big part in helping to connect so many cultures in very real and visible ways?

His name was Cândido Rondon. As a young man, he decided to join the army as an engineer. When he was only 25, he was involved in the building of a road from Rio de Janeiro to Cuiabá, a journey that previously could only be made by boat on the river. He was later given the monumental task of placing telegraph lines from Brazil to Bolivia and Peru. This was a difficult job through rough and unexplored terrain, so it required a skilled engineer. Rondon opened paths through uncharted territory, and he came into contact with the Bororo, a tribe he had family connections with on his mother's side. Rondon established a friendly and respectful relationship with the Bororo people, and the telegraph lines were completed with their help.

Next, Rondon was given the job of extending the telegraph system from Mato Grosso to the Amazon. This time he made friends with the Nambikwara, previously thought of as a timid but hostile tribe.

Rondon got to know many tribes during his expeditions, and he was a great friend to them. He was disturbed and ashamed to learn about the terrible way that they were often treated by outsiders. He fought long and hard to protect native people and their right to follow their own beliefs, traditions, and customs.

Some native people, however, still considered him an outsider. During his expeditions in Amazonia, Rondon was attacked several times, and once he was wounded by an arrow. Other members of the expedition wanted to take revenge on the people who had attacked them, but Rondon said, "Die if necessary, but never kill." Years later, Rondon set up Brazil's Indian Protection Service, an agency to safeguard the interests and support the cultures of all native peoples. Rondon's famous words became its motto.

Rondon died in 1958 and is remembered as a hero in Brazil. A state in Brazil (Rondônia) was named after him, as well as the airport in Cuiabá and several roads.

*Next week: **Abel Tasman***

3 Read the article again. Mark the sentences T (true), F (false), or DS (doesn't say).

   1 Cândido Rondon was half Portuguese and half Brazilian.

   2 Rondon was considered a good engineer.

   3 The Nambikwara were not friendly to Rondon.

   4 Rondon's motto came from one of the tribes.

   5 Many people in Brazil still appreciate what Rondon did for their country.

4 **SPEAKING** Work in pairs. Discuss the questions.

   1 What do you understand by Rondon's motto, "Die if necessary, but never kill"?

   2 What places do you know that are named after famous people?

   3 Who would you name an airport after?

GRAMMAR
The passive: verbs with two objects

1 **Check which of these three sentences is in the article on page 114. Then complete the rule by writing *person*, *direct*, and *indirect* in the spaces.**

☐ 1 They gave Rondon the job of extending the telegraph system.

☐ 2 The job of extending the telegraph system was given to Rondon.

☐ 3 Rondon was given the job of extending the telegraph system.

> **RULE:** Some verbs (like *give*, *offer*, *ask*, *promise*, *read*, *show*, *write*, *buy*, etc.) can be followed by two objects (a person and a thing).
>
> 1 verb + indirect object + direct object:
> *The teacher read the children a story.*
>
> 2 verb + direct object + indirect object:
> *The teacher read a story to the children.*
>
> So there are also two ways of making the passive construction:
>
> 1 *The **children** were read a story.*
> (¹_____ object as subject)
>
> 2 *A **story** was read to the children.*
> (²_____ object as subject)
>
> It is more usual to have the ³_____ as the subject of the passive construction, not the object.

2 **In each pair of sentences, check the one that is more usual.**

1 A A lot of money was paid to her. ☐
  B She was paid a lot of money. ☐

2 A I was told a lie. ☐
  B A lie was told to me. ☐

3 A We were promised a big party. ☐
  B A big party was promised to us. ☐

4 A I was given a new pair of shoes. ☐
  B A new pair of shoes was given to me. ☐

3 **Rewrite the sentences in your notebook using the passive. Use the person as subject.**

0 They told me a secret.
   I was told a secret.

1 They offered my mom a job.

2 People owed my dad a lot of money.

3 They gave him some medicine.

4 Someone promised us a week's vacation.

5 Someone showed me the right way to do it.

Workbook page 109

VOCABULARY
Verb + noun collocations

1 **Complete the sentences about the article on page 114 with the correct verbs.**

1 Rondon _____ friends with the Nambikwara tribe.

2 Before that, the journey could only be _____ by river transport.

3 They wanted to _____ revenge on the people who had attacked them.

4 Who could have known that his origins would _____ such a big part in connecting cultures?

2 **Put these nouns into the correct verb columns to make collocations. Some nouns can go into more than one column.**

a photo | friends | a deal | advice | a favor
a trip | a speech | an exam | a part | progress
a wish | an effort | a decision | research | money
revenge | a fool of | good | an example
a joke | advantage of | amends | a role
fun of someone | a test

make	take	play	do	give

3 **Complete each space with the correct form of one of the verbs in Exercise 2.**

When I got to the small jungle town, I ⁰ *made* friends with some of the locals and told them that I wanted to ¹_____ a trip up the river. They thought I was crazy! One of them ²_____ me some advice – he said, "Don't go! It's dangerous." At first I thought he was ³_____ fun of me, but then he ⁴_____ me some examples of the dangers I would face.
But I had ⁵_____ my decision – I wanted to explore. I had worked for years and ⁶_____ a lot of money, so I ⁷_____ a deal with three of the men to come with me.
I needed to leave soon, to ⁸_____ advantage of the good weather and to ⁹_____ as much progress as I could before the rains began. So the next morning, I put my phone in my pocket (I could use it to ¹⁰_____ photos) and got into the small boat. I looked at the river – would I make it?

4 **WRITING** **Work in pairs. Write the next paragraph of the story. Try to include more collocations from Exercise 2. Then compare with others in class.**

Workbook page 110

Literature

1 Look at the book cover and read the introduction to the extract. Do you think you would like to read the book? Why or why not?

2 Read the extract quickly and choose the best ending for the statement.

The narrator feels worried about …
1 what will happen when the sun comes up.
2 the noise of drums that he can hear.
3 the animals in the jungle around them.

The Lost World by Arthur Conan Doyle

Professor George Challenger and his friend Lord John Roxton, along with a reporter and some local guides (one of whom is named Gomez), travel up the Amazon River to find a plateau. Challenger claims he has visited the plateau before and that there are prehistoric creatures living there. Also with them is another professor who dislikes Challenger and doesn't believe his claims. The reporter narrates the story.

The very next day we did actually make our start upon this remarkable expedition. We found that all our possessions fitted very easily into the two canoes, and we divided our personnel, six in each, taking the obvious precaution, in the interests of peace, of putting one Professor into each canoe. [...]

At dawn and at sunset the monkeys screamed together and the parrots started making their high-pitched noise, but during the hot hours of the day only the loud noise of insects, like the beat of a distant surf, filled the ear, while nothing moved amongst the solemn views of huge tree-trunks, fading away into the darkness which held us in. Once some creature, an ant-eater or a bear, walked clumsily amid the shadows. It was the only sign of life which I had seen in this great Amazonian forest.

And yet there were indications that even human life itself was not far from us in those mysterious dark corners. On the third day out we were aware of a strange, deep, rhythmic beat in the air, coming and going on-and-off throughout the morning. The two boats were moving within a few yards of each other when first we heard it, and our guides remained motionless, as if they had been turned to bronze, listening intently with expressions of terror upon their faces.

"What is it, then?" I asked.

"Drums," said Lord John, carelessly, "war drums. I have heard them before."

"Yes, sir, war drums," said Gomez. "Native people, aggressive, not friendly; they watch us every mile of the way; kill us if they can."

"How can they watch us?" I asked, gazing into the dark. Gomez shrugged his broad shoulders.

"The native people know. They have their own way. They watch us. They talk the drum talk to each other. Kill us if they can."

By the afternoon of that day – my pocket diary shows me that it was Tuesday, August 18th – at least six or seven drums were beating from various points. Sometimes they beat quickly, sometimes slowly, sometimes in obvious question and answer, one far to the east breaking out in a high-pitched beat, and being followed after a pause by a deep roll from the north. There was something incredibly nerve-shaking and threatening in that constant noise, which seemed to shape itself into the words that Gomez used and endlessly repeat them: "We will kill you if we can. We will kill you if we can." No one ever moved in the silent woods. All the peace of quiet Nature lay in that dark curtain of vegetation, but away from behind there always came the one message from our fellow-man:

"We will kill you if we can," said the men in the east. "We will kill you if we can," said the men in the north. [...]

That night we tied our canoes with heavy stones for anchors in the center of the stream, and made every preparation for a possible attack. Nothing came, however, and with the dawn we pushed upon our way, the drum-beating dying out behind us.

3 ◀)) 2.36 **Read the extract again and listen. Answer the questions.**

1 Why did the two professors sit in separate boats?

2 How did the guides react when the drums started?

3 Why did the speed of the drums change from one moment to another?

4 What did the narrator think the drums were saying?

5 Why do you think they tied their canoes in the middle of the stream, not at the side?

4 VOCABULARY **Match the highlighted words in the extract with the definitions.**

1 (an unpleasant thing) suddenly starting _____

2 (moving) in an awkward, difficult way _____

3 know that something exists _____

4 looking for a long time _____

5 not moving at all _____

6 heavy things that stop a boat from moving _____

7 when the sun appears in the morning _____

8 with all one's attention _____

5 SPEAKING **Work in pairs. Discuss the questions.**

1 What do you think the people who were drumming were actually "saying" to each other?

2 Lord John isn't worried by the drums, but the guides are. How do you think you would feel if you were part of the expedition? Give reasons.

WRITING
A short biography

1 Read Joel's biography of Oliver Tambo and answer the questions.

1 What did Tambo study during his life?

2 Where did he live, apart from in South Africa?

3 Why did he give the ANC presidency to Nelson Mandela?

2 Which paragraph is which? Write letters in the boxes.

A Conclusion

B Early life

C Introduction to the person

D Main achievements

3 You're going to write a short biography.

1 Think of something in your country (e.g., a street, an airport, a square) that has the name of a famous person.

2 Make notes about the person's life. Do research on the Internet if you need to.

3 Decide which information is most important to include in a biography.

4 Now write the biography.

- Make sure that you include information that makes it clear why the place was named after the person.

- Follow the structure of the biography about Tambo.

- Write 150–200 words.

☐ Johannesburg is my home city, and the international airport here is called O.R. Tambo Airport. It is named after Oliver Tambo, who not many people know much about – almost everyone has heard of Nelson Mandela, but Tambo is not as well known around the world.

☐ Oliver Reginald Tambo (everyone knew him as O.R.) was born in 1917 in an area of South Africa now known as the Eastern Cape. As a young man he studied education, and for a while he was a teacher. Later, he gave up teaching to study law, and in 1952 he joined Nelson Mandela's law firm.

☐ These were the years of apartheid in South Africa. Tambo, like Mandela, was part of the African National Congress (ANC), which was an illegal organization at that time. Mandela was sent to prison on Robben Island, and Tambo left the country. He lived at different times in Zambia and in London. He was the "president in exile" of the ANC and worked very hard to get support from other countries in the struggle to end apartheid.

☐ He went back to South Africa in 1990 when the ANC became legal. But he had a stroke and could not work any longer, so he passed the presidency of the ANC to Mandela. Tambo died in 1993, before he could see the first black government of his country. In 2006 the airport was renamed after him to honor his achievements. And to sum up, I think that this honor rightly recognized the very important role that Tambo played in the development of the country he loved.

SPEAKING

Part 3: Collaborative task

Workbook page 107

1   Imagine your school is organizing a week's trip for the students in your grade. Here are some ideas for some of the places they could take you and a question to discuss. First, you have some time to look at the task.

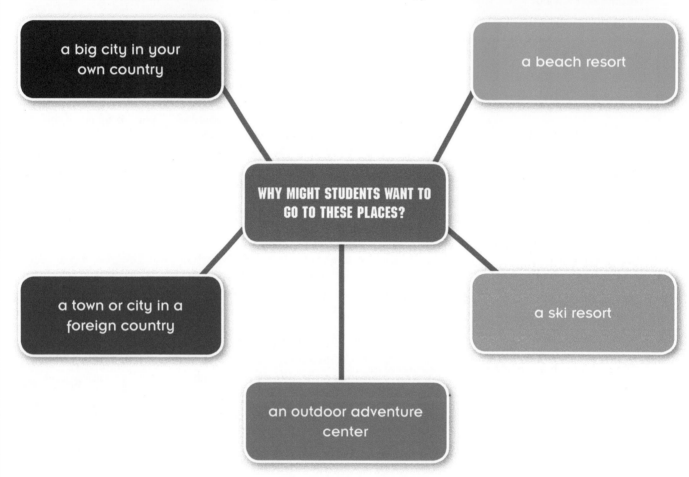

a big city in your own country

a beach resort

WHY MIGHT STUDENTS WANT TO GO TO THESE PLACES?

a town or city in a foreign country

a ski resort

an outdoor adventure center

Now talk to each other about why students might want to go to these places. Then decide which would be the best place to go on a school trip.

Part 4: Follow-up discussion

2   **Discuss the following questions.**

Workbook page 115

1   Do you think it's important for schools to offer trips like these? Why or why not?

2   What things can students learn on trips like these?

3   What might students find hardest about going away for a week?

4   What might students enjoy most about going away for a week?

5   Some people say that school trips are expensive and discriminate against children whose parents don't have the money to pay for them. What do you think?

6   Are school trips more useful for learning about some school subjects, e.g., foreign languages, than others? What other subjects can you learn about on school trips? Explain how.

VOCABULARY

1 **Complete the sentences with the words in the list. There are four extra words.**

waterfall | far-fetched | squeezing | make | volcano | reef | took | solar
gave | bonus | action-packed | breathtaking | do | star

1 My baby cousin drew a picture of me by _____ toothpaste onto the mirror in the bathroom.
2 Jack has an image of the _____ system projected on the ceiling of his bedroom.
3 The effect of the fireworks and the music was really _____ .
4 Flights were disrupted when a _____ erupted and filled the sky with ash.
5 We climbed up to the top of the _____ and watched the water pouring down.
6 The water in the bay is always calm because it's protected by a _____ .
7 Pete's dad gave him some good advice, but I don't think Pete _____ it.
8 We weren't expecting good weather on our vacation, so the sunshine was a real _____ .
9 Ann's presentation is next week, so she needs to _____ some research.
10 His excuse for being late was so _____ that I didn't believe a word of it.

/10

GRAMMAR

2 **Complete the sentences with the phrases in the list. There are two extra phrases.**

must have | due to | was given | consequently | to have | must be | can't have | to be

1 Johnny Depp is known _____ earned $50 million for just one movie.
2 Alan was always eating junk food, and _____ , he put on a lot of weight.
3 Silvia is a terrible singer – she _____ won the singing competition!
4 New York is known _____ one of the most expensive cities in the world.
5 Janet left half an hour ago; she _____ home by now.
6 Luis _____ two identical sweaters for his birthday.

3 **Find and correct the mistake in each sentence.**

1 I'm sure a lot of people have met the new boy. Sue mustn't be the only one.
2 Only a few people are thought to have survive so long alone in the desert.
3 Oh no, I'm going to got this all wrong. I didn't understand the question.
4 My father was brought up by his aunt after his parents were died.
5 Kelly Jones is know for being very generous.
6 I suppose it's possible – Carol might be at the party last night, but I didn't see her.

/12

FUNCTIONAL LANGUAGE

4 **Choose the correct options.**

1 A I've lost my phone! I *can / must* have left it on the bus.
   B Oh *no / shame*, that is a problem.
2 A Last weekend we couldn't find our cat. We thought she *was / had been* run over by a car.
   B How *shame / terrible*! You must have been very worried.
3 A You know, in the past, being left-handed was *believed / known* to be unnatural.
   B That *mustn't / can't* have been easy for left-handed people.
4 A In some countries black cats are *thought / known* to be unlucky.
   B Yes, but in other countries they are *seen / looked at* as bringers of good luck.

/8

MY SCORE | /30

| 22 – 30 |
| 10 – 21 |
| 0 – 9 |

PRONUNCIATION

UNIT 1

Diphthongs: alternative spellings

1 🔊 1.07 **Read and listen to the sentences. Notice the different spellings of the same sound.**

1 My dad **might** have **died cli_mbing** on the **ice**.
2 Joe **tipt_oed** alone through the **snow**, **though**.
3 We **stayed late**. When it **rained**, we went **away**.
4 She **found** the m**ou**ntain **out** of **town**.
5 The **boys enj_oyed** the **noise** as the water **boiled**.

2 🔊 1.08 **Listen, repeat, and practice.**

UNIT 2

Phrasal verb stress

1 🔊 1.13 **Read and listen to the dialogue below.**

GILLIAN Moving to France when I was nine was tough. It turned out all right, though.

SAM How did you pick up French?

GILLIAN I hung out with my French friends.

SAM Do you ever run into them?

GILLIAN Run into them? I don't live in France anymore!

2 (Circle) **the correct words.**

Red indicates ¹*primary / secondary* stress. Blue indicates ²*primary / secondary* stress. In two-part phrasal verbs, primary stress is usually on the ³*verb / particle* and secondary stress is on the ⁴*verb / particle*.

3 🔊 1.14 **Listen, repeat, and practice.**

UNIT 3

Adding emphasis with *so, such, do,* or *did*

1 🔊 1.18 **Read and listen to the dialogue.**

MILLIE It was **such** a great match.
ROB I know! It was **so** exciting!
MILLIE Lee lost, but she **did** play well.
ROB I agree. I **do** think she tried her best.

2 🔊 1.18 **Listen again. What is the effect of the words in bold?**

3 🔊 1.19 **Listen, repeat, and practice.**

UNIT 4

Pronouncing words with *gh*

1 🔊 1.23 **Read and listen to the extracts from Answers4U. What do you notice about the pronunciation of *gh* in the words in bold?**

PAUL At first, I **thought** it would be easy. But now I'm scared I'll only get **through** it with a lot of problems.

SARAH Actually, the only "box" is the way we've been **brought** up to see problems. Try to stop seeing things as "**right**" or "wrong." If you try an idea and other people **laugh** at it, that's their problem, not yours. Anyway, **enough** from me. I hope these ideas help!

2 🔊 1.24 **Listen, repeat, and practice.**

UNIT 5

The /ə/ sound

1 🔊 1.29 **Read and listen to this message. Which sound do the words in blue share?**

Thank you for calling the Computer Now Helpline. To find out how to zip a file, upgrade a system, or stream a video, press 1. To learn how to connect to Wi-Fi, browse the Internet, or post an update, press 2. For all other inquiries, press 3.

2 🔊 1.30 **Listen, repeat, and practice.**

UNIT 6

The /tʃ/ sound: negative auxiliaries + *you*

1 🔊 1.33 **Complete the sentences with the words in the list.**

aren't | can't | didn't | couldn't
wouldn't | haven't

0 You're going to the party, _____*aren't*_____ you?
1 You can play the piano, _____ you?
2 You could understand it, _____ you?
3 You would volunteer, _____ you?
4 You've already finished, _____ you?
5 You made this mess, _____ you?

2 🔊 1.34 **Listen, check, and repeat with a partner.**

UNIT 7

Intonation: encouraging someone

1 🔊 2.06 **Read and listen to the dialogue.**

BECKY   Hi, Harry! Oh, you don't look very happy. What's wrong?

HARRY   Well … I just failed my driving test.

BECKY   That's too bad, but **don't let it get you down.** A lot of people fail the first time!

HARRY   Actually, it's not the first time.

BECKY   Oh well, **look on the bright side** – you can only get better!

HARRY   I guess so … I just feel kind of stupid.

BECKY   **It'll be all right!** You just need to practice more, that's all. **I know you can do it!**

2 🔊 2.06 **Draw arrows above the blue phrases to show how Becky's voice goes up and down.**

3 🔊 2.07 **Listen, repeat, and practice.**

UNIT 8

Weak forms with past modals

1 🔊 2.11 **Read and listen to the dialogue.**

KIM   Oh no! I forgot Mom's birthday! I <u>would've remembered</u> if I didn't have all these exams!

NELLIE   Really, Kim … you <u>could've written</u> it on your calendar.

KIM   I <u>could've done</u> many things, Nellie. But that's not the point.

NELLIE   You <u>should've asked</u> your dad to remind you! What are you going to do?

2 🔊 2.11 **Listen again and** (circle) **the word in blue in which the /v/ sound in 've *is* pronounced. Why do you think this might be?**

3 🔊 2.12 **Listen, repeat, and practice.**

UNIT 9

The /tən/ word ending

1 🔊 2.15 **Complete the sentences with the words in the list.**

~~gotten~~ | written | kitten | mitten | bitten | rotten

0   Pam should've _____*gotten*_____ home earlier.

1   The firefighter rescued the _____ .

2   The _____ onion smells.

3   Lee was _____ by a spider yesterday.

4   Jenny lost a _____ in the snow.

5   It should be _____ down.

2 🔊 2.16 **Listen, check, and repeat with a partner.**

UNIT 10

Linking: omission of the /h/ sound

1 🔊 2.20 **Read and listen to the dialogue.**

HELEN   Hilary and Harry aren't speaking to each other.

HUGO   What happened?

HELEN   He hurt her feelings. He said he didn't like her new haircut.

HUGO   How horrible! Did he mean to upset her?

HELEN   Of course he didn't!

2 🔊 2.20 **Listen again and** <u>underline</u> **the words in which the letter *h* is silent. Is it silent in stressed or unstressed words?**

3 🔊 2.21 **Listen, repeat, and practice.**

UNIT 11

Sentence stress: modals for speculation

1 🔊 2.27 **Read and listen to the dialogue.**

GINA   I just watched a TV show that said aliens <u>might have visited</u> Earth.

NED   Well … they <u>might have, I suppose</u>.

GINA   It said that they <u>may have built the pyramids</u>!

NED   It <u>could be true</u> – if they had the technology to get here in the first place.

GINA   In fact, they <u>may be in our town</u> right now!

2 🔊 2.27 **Listen again, and color the box black above the word with the main stress.**

3 🔊 2.28 **Listen, repeat, and practice.**

UNIT 12

Flapping *t* and *d*

1 🔊 2.34 **Listen and** (circle) **the word that completes each sentence.**

0   It was sold to the highest (bidder) / batter.

1   The bike's *metal / pedal* is broken.

2   The rose *petal / medal* smelled sweet.

3   She won the gold *matter / medal* in swimming.

4   Some baseball bats are made of *metal / matter*.

5   It doesn't *pedal / matter*.

2 🔊 2.35 **Listen, check, and repeat with a partner.**

3 **How are *t* and *d* pronounced in the italicized words?**

GET IT RIGHT!

UNIT 1

Verb patterns

> **Learners often use the wrong verb form after certain verbs, using the gerund instead of infinitive and vice versa.**
>
> ✓ *I'm looking forward to* **going** *to the festival.*
> ✗ *I'm looking forward* ~~to go~~ *to the festival.*

Check (✓) the correct sentences and write an X (✗) next to the incorrect ones. Rewrite the incorrect ones correctly in your notebook.

0   Ben was looking forward to climb the cliff.   ✗
    Ben was looking forward to climbing the cliff.

1   They wanted go sailing, but the weather conditions were too extreme.   ☐

2   I enjoy to wander around outdoor markets when I'm on vacation.   ☐

3   Jo refused to swing across the river on the rope.   ☐

4   Do you think you'll manage completing the climb?   ☐

5   Tim doesn't mind helping out on the mountaineering course on weekends.   ☐

6   Kate hoped to reach the glacier but slipped.   ☐

7   The children learned to build a shelter during the survival course.   ☐

8   Megan was thrilled when she got her exam results since she'd expected to fail.   ☐

remember, try, stop, regret, and forget

> **Learners often use the wrong verb form after the verbs *remember*, *try*, *stop*, *regret*, and *forget*, which can all be used with both the gerund and infinitive but with different meanings.**
>
> ✓ *I really think you should stop* **smoking**.
> ✗ *I really think you should* ~~stop to smoke~~.

Choose the correct verb form.

1   Did you remember *buying / to buy* some milk?

2   John stopped *getting / to get* a soda at a café on the way to the beach.

3   I will never forget *climbing / to climb* Everest. It was the ultimate experience.

4   Kathryn tried *climbing / to climb* Everest three times but never succeeded.

5   Dan stopped *studying / to study* after the exam.

6   They regretted *going / to go* to the party because they didn't know anyone and felt awkward.

7   Dad tried *completing / to complete* the crossword, but it was impossible.

8   I regret *informing / to inform* you that there are no seats available on that flight.

UNIT 2

that and *which* in relative clauses

> **Learners often use *that* instead of *which* in non-defining relative clauses.**
>
> ✓ *Working leads to self-esteem,* **which** *is vital for a happy life.*
> ✗ *Working leads to self-esteem,* ~~that~~ *is vital for a happy life.*

Match the two parts of the sentences and rewrite them as one sentence using either *that* or *which*. Use *that* where possible.

0   The Arctic tern flies about 70,000 miles,   *b*

1   The grey whale is the animal   ☐

2   Domenico Lucano had an idea   ☐

3   Our teacher always praises us when we've done well on a test,   ☐

4   I spoke to him in Italian,   ☐

5   Elana has decided to live abroad,   ☐

a   helps give us confidence.

b   is an amazing distance.

c   swims about 18,000 km every year.

d   I think is very brave of her.

e   saved his village.

f   I had learned while working in Rome.

0   *The Arctic tern flies about 70,000 miles, which is an amazing distance.*

Relative pronouns

> Learners often omit relative pronouns in defining relative clauses when you can't.
>
> ✓ I don't know any people **who** went to the festival.
> ✗ I don't know any ~~people went~~ to the festival.

Check (✓) the correct sentences and write an X (✗) next to the incorrect ones. Rewrite the incorrect ones correctly in your notebook.

0 Did you run into any of the people usually play there on Mondays? ☒
   Did you run into any of the people who usually play there on Mondays?

1 The pedestrians crossed the road had to run to avoid being hit by the car. ☐

2 Martha said she would arrive at noon. ☐

3 They went through a bad time lasted a few months. ☐

4 Who is the man is waving at us? ☐

5 It's a problem residents have dealt with for years. ☐

6 The Tuareg are the people regularly cross national borders. ☐

UNIT 3

much vs. many

> Learners often confuse *much* and *many*.
>
> ✓ There are **many** more advantages than disadvantages.
> ✗ There are ~~much~~ more advantages than disadvantages.
>
> ✓ There was **much** more information on the website.
> ✗ There was ~~many~~ more information on the website.

Complete the sentences with *much* or *many*.

1 There wouldn't be so _____ disobedient children if parents were stricter.

2 I can spend as _____ time as necessary making the costume.

3 She should ask Mrs. Davies for advice. She knows so _____ about parenting.

4 The book contains _____ useful ideas about bringing up children well.

5 You should come inside now. You've already spent too _____ time in the sun.

6 There is _____ more to be said about this, but we don't have time now.

most

> Learner often make the mistake of adding *the* before *most* or including *of* after *most*.
>
> ✓ **Most** drivers are careless.
> ✗ ~~The~~ most drivers are careless.
>
> ✓ **Most** parents find raising children a challenge.
> ✗ Most ~~of~~ parents find raising children a challenge.

Check (✓) the correct sentences and write an X (✗) next to the incorrect ones. Rewrite the incorrect ones correctly in your notebook.

1 The most of my teachers at school were very strict. ☐

2 Most of my friends use their phones a lot. ☐

3 James spent most of the time I was there getting ready for the party. ☐

4 Sally tried on a few outfits, but the most of them were too big for her. ☐

5 It would be interesting to know if most of people agreed with Amy Chua's ideas. ☐

6 Were the most of your old school friends at the reunion? ☐

UNIT 4

used to vs. would

> Learners often make mistakes with *used to* and *would*. While *used to* is used with both action and stative verbs, *would* is only used with action verbs.
>
> ✓ We **used to walk** a lot.
> ✓ We **would walk** a lot.
> ✓ You **used to be** happy.
> ✗ ~~We would be happy.~~

Complete the sentence with *used to* or *would*. In some cases, both answers are possible.

1 He _____ be very bad tempered, but he's nicer now.

2 The man who _____ live there moved to Spain.

3 When my grandma was in school, she _____ play outside.

4 Laura _____ watch a lot of TV before she went to college.

5 Mom and Dad _____ look younger 15 years ago.

6 They _____ have a lot of toys. Now they have a lot of books.

UNIT 5
should

> **Learners often use would, can, and must instead of should.**
>
> ✓ Lots of people think that animals **should** be free.
> ✗ Lots of people think that animals ~~must~~ be free.

For each pair of sentences check (✓) the correct one.

1. a ☐ Your computer is very slow. I think you must upgrade your system.

   b ☐ Your computer is very slow. I think you should upgrade your system.

2. a ☐ Sally wouldn't have emigrated if she hadn't been unhappy here.

   b ☐ Sally shouldn't have emigrated if she hadn't been unhappy here.

3. a ☐ Our teachers should motivate us to study more so we do better on exams.

   b ☐ Our teachers would motivate us to study more so we do better on exams.

4. a ☐ We should launch the new product before the end of the month, or we won't hit the sales figures. We have no option.

   b ☐ We must launch the new product before the end of the month, or we won't hit the sales figures. We have no option.

UNIT 6
Comparatives

> **Learners often use the comparative instead of the superlative and vice versa.**
>
> ✓ That was the **worst** evening of my vacation.
> ✗ That was the ~~worse~~ evening of my vacation.
> ✓ Their behavior seems to be getting **worse**.
> ✗ Their behavior seems to be getting ~~worst~~.

Complete the sentences with the correct superlative or comparative in the list.

happier | happiest | harder | hardest
higher | highest | better | best

1. The _____ the questions, the more money can be won by the participants.

2. What's the _____ way to ask someone out?

3. When Liz got married, it was the _____ day of her life.

4. The _____ the salary, the more money you can spend.

5. The exam I had yesterday was the _____ one I've ever taken.

6. Luke and Sally's engagement party would have been _____ if they'd invited more people.

7. Tom decided to climb the _____ mountain in Scotland.

8. Some people think that the richer you are the _____ you are.

Linkers of contrast

> **Learners often confuse linkers or make mistakes with form.**
>
> ✓ **Although** I studied a lot, I still failed the exam.
> ✗ ~~Despite~~ I studied a lot, I still failed the exam.

Rewrite the sentences either by using a different linker or by changing the form in your notebook.

0. In spite they got engaged, they never got married.
   Although they got engaged, they never got married.
   In spite of getting engaged, they never got married.

1. Even though confessing to the crime, the police didn't arrest her.

2. We made an inquiry about the delivery. Despite, no one got back to us.

3. Nevertheless the fact that they made a complaint about the food, the chef didn't apologize.

4. The children took the move to the city well despite they had been happy living in the town.

UNIT 7
Future continuous

> **Learners often use the present continuous when the future continuous is more commonly used.**
>
> ✓ On our vacation we **will be staying** in tents.
> ✗ On our vacation we ~~are staying~~ in tents.

Check (✓) the correct sentences and write an X (✗) next to the incorrect ones. Rewrite the incorrect ones correctly in your notebook.

1. At this time tomorrow we are exercising at the gym. ☐

2. I am seeing you sometime over the weekend, so I'll show you then. ☐

3. When we meet, I'll be wearing a black dress and a hat. ☐

4. I'll come to the airport to pick you up. I'm waiting for you at arrivals. ☐

5. This time next week they will lie on a beach relaxing. ☐

UNIT 8
would

> Learners often use *would* in the *if* clause of conditional sentences instead of using a present, simple past, or past perfect form.
>
> ✓ *Don't hesitate to contact me if you **need** any more information.*
> ✗ *Don't hesitate to contact me if you ~~would~~ need any more information.*
>
> ✓ *If you **had come** to the park, you would have enjoyed yourself.*
> ✗ *If you ~~would have~~ come to the park, you would have enjoyed yourself.*

Put the words in order to make sentences. In each sentence there is an extra word that you don't need.

1 If / would / checked / the / mistake / calculations / they / they / would / have / realized / had / their / .

   _____

2 cookbook / The / wouldn't / meal / wouldn't / turned out / lent / so well / if / you / hadn't / me / have / your / .

   _____

3 would / 'll / that / She / do / her / provided / we / help / it / .

   _____

4 get / infection / you / hands / might / don't / would / wash / If / your / you / an / .

   _____

5 The / wouldn't / been / have / ripped / would / it / had / cloth / if / stronger / .

   _____

6 as / time / won't / It / problem / long / a / as / would / arrive / on / be / you / .

   _____

UNIT 9
wish

> Learners often use *wish* when *hope* or *want* are required and vice versa.
>
> ✓ *I **want** my children to live in a happy family.*
> ✗ *I ~~wish~~ my children to live in a happy family.*

Choose the correct verb.

1 Chloe *hopes / wishes* you hadn't told her about Richard.
2 I *wish / hope* you have a good time in Madrid.
3 Dad *wishes / wants* to learn how to play the piano.
4 We *want / wish* our neighbor didn't play the violin.
5 Steve *hopes / wishes* to take a math course next year.
6 I *hope / wish* that you enjoyed the play.
7 I'm having a BBQ on Saturday, and I *hope / wish* you can come.

I wish / If only

> Learners often use the simple past instead of the past perfect after *I wish / If only* when talking about the past.
>
> ✓ *I wish I **had gone** to the party.*
> ✗ *I wish I ~~went~~ to the party.*

Match the two parts of the sentences.

1 I wish we won
2 I wish we had won
3 Tom's mom wishes he had studied harder
4 Tom's mom wishes he studied harder
5 If only I had slept until later,
6 If only I didn't sleep so late,
7 If only Pete hadn't let you down,
8 If only Pete didn't let you down

a at school so he could get into college.
b all the time, you'd be friends.
c a game occasionally. It would be nice!
d I wouldn't be so tired now.
e you'd still be friends.
f the game. Everyone was so disappointed.
g at school and got into college.
h I'd have more time in the mornings.

UNIT 10
Reported speech

> **Learners often omit *if* when reporting *yes/no* questions or use the auxiliary *do* when it isn't needed in reported questions. Learners also need to be careful with word order.**
>
> ✓ *He asked me **if** I wanted to go.*
> ✗ *He asked me ~~did I want~~ to go.*
>
> ✓ *The teacher asked me how old **I was**.*
> ✗ *The teacher asked me how old ~~was I~~.*

Rewrite these incorrect sentences correctly.

1 Simon asked me did I remember to pass on the message to the class.

   _____

   _____

2 Sandra asked how efficiently worked the machine.

   _____

3 The students asked the speaker how big had been the impact of war.

   _____

   _____

UNIT 11
Cause and effect linkers

> **Learners often make mistakes with cause and effect linkers: *so, consequently, because, because of, due to, as a result*.**
>
> ✓ *Fish can breathe under water **because** they have gills.*
> ✗ *Fish can breathe under water ~~because of~~ they have gills.*

Choose the correct linker.

1 *Consequently / Due to / Because* the movie's success, the director was in high demand.
2 Many people witnessed the solar eclipse. *Due to / Because of / As a result*, a number of people were admitted to hospitals with eye damage.
3 It's a very popular tourist destination *because of / as a result / due* its breathtaking views.
4 Emily spent all her money on shoes and *because / consequently / due to* had no money to buy jeans.
5 I really hate being interrupted *because / so / consequently* please wait for me to finish speaking!
6 Daniela's dad was angry *as a result / for / because of* her disappointing grades.

UNIT 12
been and *being*

> **Learners often confuse *been* and *being*.**
>
> ✓ *I don't think your talent is **being** recognized.*
> ✗ *I don't think your talent is ~~been~~ recognized.*
>
> ✓ *I've always **been** able to rely on him.*
> ✗ *I've always ~~being~~ able to rely on him.*

Choose the correct form, *been* or *being*.

1 Work on the school is *being / been* done at the moment.
2 Advances are *being / been* made all the time in medical research.
3 Police have *being / been* trying to determine what happened during the burglary.
4 Richard feels like he has *being / been* taken advantage of.
5 The patient is *being / been* transferred to a different hospital at the moment.
6 Since we played the joke on him, he's *being / been* avoiding us.

UNIT 6, PAGE 56

Student A

You are an 18-year-old student who suffers from claustrophobia (which means you really don't like enclosed spaces). You can be in an elevator for three or four minutes, but after that you panic and need to get out as soon as possible. When you are stressed, you usually sing to help you relax.

Student C

You are a middle-aged lawyer. You have work to do in your office, and you think it's very important that you get to your office soon. You are not a very patient person. You do not like students or unemployed people very much, and you absolutely hate music.

STUDENTS B & D

Student B

You are an elderly person, about 65 years old. You have been in situations like this before, so you aren't worried. However, you have an important appointment with your doctor in an hour's time, so you really need to get out as soon as possible. You would like the other people to do something practical to fix the situation.

Student D

You are an unemployed person in your twenties. You are in the elevator because you are going to a job interview that starts in 30 minutes. But it's not a job you really want, so you are not very worried. Also, you are a very calm person, and you enjoy helping other people. You also enjoy singing.